AUSCHWITZ

BIRKENAU
AUSCHWITZ II
SS HEADQUARTERS
RAILYARD
LIGHT
INDUSTRY
AUSCHWITZ I

AUSCHWITZ

Adam Bujak
Photographs

Teresa and Henryk
Świebocki
Text

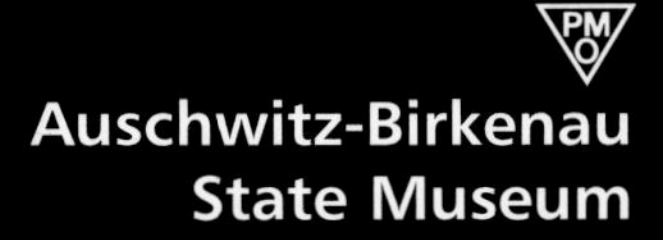

Auschwitz-Birkenau
State Museum

Biały Kruk

THE RESIDENCE OF DEATH

Published in cooperation with
The Foundation to Commemorate the Victims
of the Auschwitz – Birkenau Death Camp in Oświęcim

Edited by
Teresa and Henryk Świebocki

Translated by
William Brand

Designed and co-edited by
Leszek Sosnowski

Desktop Publishing
Biały Kruk Studio
Wojciech Bartkowski
Sebastian Stachowski

All quotes of camp commandant Rudolf Höss were translated by Constantine Fitzgibbon in *KL Auschwitz Seen by the SS*, Oświęcim 1997
All quotes of Pery Broad were translated by Krystyna Michalik in *KL Auschwitz Seen by the SS*, Oświęcim 1997
Other quotations accompanying the illustrations come from: Archives of the Auschwitz-Birkenau State Museum; *Wśród koszmarnej zbrodni*. Ed. Jadwiga Bezwińska, Danuta Czech, Oświęcim 1975; *London has been informed. Reports by Auschwitz escapees.* Ed. Henryk Świebocki, Oświęcim 1997; Zofia Kossak, *Z otchłani*

Black and White Photographs and documents
The Archives of the Auschwitz – Birkenau State Museum

Published in Polish, English, German, Italian, French, and Spanish

Lithography
Pasaż, Kraków

First Edition, Kraków – Oświęcim 2003

ISBN 83-88918-26-5

Photo on page 2.
Auschwitz I and Auschwitz II-Birkenau concentration camps. Allied aerial reconnaissance photograph from June 26, 1944. This photograph was analyzed and described by the American researchers Dino A. Brugioni and Robert G. Poirier (Photograph from the collections of the National Archives, Washington).

Historical Introduction

"...we realized then for the first time
that there were no words to express that contempt,
that destruction of human beings."

The largest of the death camps

The site of Auschwitz-Birkenau, the Nazi death camp in Oświęcim, is the best known place of martyrdom and destruction in the world. This camp has become a symbol of the Holocaust, of genocide and terror, of the violation of basic human rights and of what racism, antisemitism, xenophobia, chauvinism, and intolerance can lead to. The name of the camp has become a sort of cultural code that defines the most negative interpersonal relations. It is a synonym for the breakdown of contemporary civilization and culture.

The Nazis created many different kinds of camps in occupied Europe, but Auschwitz has become the best known of them all. Several factors account for this, including the enormous number of victims and the vast area that the camp covered, as well as the fact that the crimes committed here were already fairly well known during the war. A relatively high proportion of prisoners survived Auschwitz in comparison to other death camps. After the war, these survivors were active in efforts to commemorate the victims and share the truth about the story of the camp.

The camp had several functions and its history is complex. For this reason, Auschwitz has both a universal significance, and significances associated with the memories and histories of the peoples who became its victims. It was the largest center for the mass extermination of the European Jews and, at the same time, the largest concentration camp for prisoners of other nationalities. It was a place of slave labor, of executions and criminal medical experiments, and of plunder on a gigantic scale.

The Nazis sent to Auschwitz at least 1,100,000 Jews from various European countries, nearly 150,000 Poles, mostly political prisoners, approximately 23,000 Roma from several European countries, 15,000 Soviet prisoners of war, and 25,000 prisoners of other nationalities—Czech, French, Yugoslavian, Russian, Byelorussian, and Ukrainian.

The Nazi Vision of a "New Europe"

The founding of the camp and its operation were inextricably linked with Nazi ideology and policies. The years before the outbreak of the Second World War were a prelude to what happened later. "We have given the German nation new ideals," Adolf Hitler stated after taking power in 1933. The fundamental elements in the Nazi ideology were hatred of democracy, Marxism, and Jews, along with the conviction that the Germans were a nation set above other nations, that Nordic blood was the best blood, and that Germany was superior to anything else. This ideology aimed at creating a society from which all those who did not meet the definition of "racially pure" Germans would be eliminated. The Jews were the main target of this elimination, but it also extended to other groups, including the handicapped and the Sinti and Roma (Gypsy people).

The idea of the superiority of the "Aryan" race and the exceptionality of the Germans was linked to a drive for territorial expansion. After Hitler's seizure of power, both domestic and foreign policy in Germany were subordinated to realizing all these aims. At a secret meeting with the Third Reich military leadership and foreign minister in November 1937, two years before the outbreak of the Second World War, Hitler said that "in our case, it is a matter of acquiring not population, but only space suitable for agriculture".[1]

The Nazi party program defined these intentions with equal clarity: "We demand land and soil (colonies) to feed our nation and settle the overflow of our population".[2]

In a speech to the generals ten days before the outbreak of the Second World War, Hitler said: "I have given orders and ordered the shooting of anyone who utters even a single word criticizing the fact that the goal of the war is not reaching some set line, but the physical destruction of the enemy. To this goal, only in the East for the moment, I have prepared my Death's Head units, ordering them to kill . . . men, women and children of Polish origin or who speak Polish, without mercy. Only in this way will we acquire the living space that we need . . . Poland will be depopulated and settled by Germans".[3]

The war and its first results

After the German attack on Poland on September 1, 1939, and the Soviet attack on September 17, came the division of Poland, part of which was annexed to the Third Reich. The central part of Poland was formed into the so-called General Government, completely subject to the Germans and administered by the Nazi administrative-police apparatus. Under the terms of a secret German-Soviet agreement on August 1939, the eastern part was annexed by the Soviet Union and only came under German occupation in 1941, after the outbreak of war between Germany and the USSR.

At the beginning of the war, Hitler ordered the murder of all the physically handicapped people in Germany, and of those regarded as mentally ill. Special commissions of physicians determined who should be killed. These people were sent to six euthanasia centers in the Third Reich, where they were put to death in gas chambers constructed especially for this purpose. This operation foreshadowed the later mass-scale extermination operations that the Nazis carried out in occupied Poland.

After the taking of Poland and subsequent attacks and the conquest of other countries, a significant part of Europe lay under Nazi occupation. The Germans had occupied Bohemia and Moravia even before the war. The German army attacked Denmark and Norway in April 1940, Belgium, the Netherlands, and France in May, Yugoslavia and Greece in April 1941, and its recent ally, the Soviet Union, in June 1941.

The first years of the war saw enormous German success. Country after country fell under Nazi occupation. Other countries were allies of Germany or found themselves in the Third Reich's sphere of influence. To a greater or lesser degree, they cooperated with the Germans and carried out Nazi policy.

The Nazis regarded parts of the population in the occupied countries as inferior races, less worthy and fated to rapid destruction during the war or to gradual extermination. Various plans arose, ranging from forced resettlement to mass sterilization and physical liquidation. In 1942, Himmler stated explicitly that "our task is not the germanization of the East in the old sense of that word... we want, instead, to make sure that purely German people, of German blood, actually live in the East."[4]

The so-called General Plan East (General Plan Ost), developed under Himmler's direct supervision, envisioned the movement of the ethnic borders of the Reich some 1,000 kilometers to the east and the designation of the territory thus acquired for German colonists. The local population, the Slavs and other peoples, were to be resettled beyond the Urals or partially eradicated. Such an operation was planned for 80 to 85% of the Poles.

"The Jewish Question" and the fate of other "subhumans"

The most tragic fate fell on the European Jews. Under the plan for the total destruction of this people, which the Nazis referred to as "the final solution of the Jewish question," they were to be completely isolated from the remainder of the population and then, while the war was still on, murdered. Slavs, mainly the Poles and the Russians, including Russian prisoners of war, were also victims of the Nazis, but their destruction was to take a different course. The Jews were distinguished from other victims by being deprived of the fundamental right to life, of existence—the most basic of human rights. They were not murdered for joining the resistance movement or for belonging to a party or organization, but solely for having been born Jewish. Membership in a given "race" became the sole criterion for destruction. Elie Wiesel, a former Auschwitz prisoner and winner of the Nobel Peace Prize, has noted succinctly that while not all victims of Nazism were Jews, all Jews were victims.

Many utterances by the German leadership refer to the Nazi policies. Otto Thierack, justice minister of the Third Reich, specified the goals to be met while the war was still on: "The German people should be totally freed of Poles, Russians, Jews, and Gypsies" [5], while Hans Frank, the Third Reich's governor in occupied Poland, stated clearly that the Jews were a race that must be completely exterminated.

Before the war, the largest percentage of Jews (in proportion to the general population) lived in Poland. Jews had lived in this country since the Middle Ages, maintaining and developing their own forms of religious life, a rich culture, and their own customs. Some of them had assimilated into Polish society and played an active role in cultural and political life. More than three million Jews lived in Poland, making up ten percent of that country's population and constituting a quarter of all the Jews in Europe.

The Wannsee Conference: Institutionalized extermination

On January 20, 1942, Reinhard Heydrich, chief of the Security Police and Security Service, chaired a secret conference in Berlin-Wannsee. High officials from the Third Reich ministries of the interior, foreign affairs, justice, and eastern lands attended, along with officials from the General Government, the Reich chancellery, the Nazi party chancellery, and the main SS offices. The subject of the conference was the coordination of the work of all offices and institutions in carrying out plans for the total extermination of eleven million European Jews. In reality, however, the extermination had already begun. Deportations of Jews to ghettos in occupied Poland had been underway for two years, and mass murder operations (by shooting) had begun in the western part of the Soviet Union as soon as the Germans attacked that country in the summer of 1941. Gas had already begun to be used to put people to death in the Chełmno nad Nerem (Kulmhof) and Auschwitz camps. The conference approved overall guidelines and specified, among other things, procedures for "combing" all of Europe from west to east in order to apprehend all the Jews fated for destruction.

A list attached to the conference protocols contained precise figures on eleven million Jews living not only in countries occupied by the Germans, but also in the satellite countries and the countries that the Germans planned to conquer, such as Britain. The list counted both the many millions of Jews in Eastern Europe and the several hundred in Albania. It indicates that no Jewish community on European territory was to be spared.

An analysis of this list clearly indicates one of the reasons that the mass extermination centers were set up in the East. It would be far easier to transport thousands or even hundreds of thousands of people from Western or Southern Europe to the East, than to transport millions of Jews elsewhere from Poland and the occupied USSR. This is why Western Europe did not become the scene of the mass extermination of the Jews. It was, however, the place where they were concentrated and deported to the East through assembly camps such as Drancy in France, Malines in Belgium, and Westerbork in the Netherlands.

Another factor influencing the location of the death camps in occupied Poland was the fact that the Germans treated that country as a colony, and therefore felt no need to take public opinion into account or to conceal the crime. The Germans applied particularly harsh, ruthless terror against the Poles. The streets were constantly plastered with announcements of executions and reprisals for violating the orders and regulations of the occupation regime.

Nazi policy in occupied Poland

At the beginning of the German occupation of Poland, the Nazi authorities were not yet focused on plans for the physical destruction of the Jews, in relation to whom various solutions, including plans for forced resettlement, were proposed. On the other hand, the introduction of the so-called "new order," aimed at completely subjugating the Polish population through regulations and internal policies, was in full swing.

Above all, the Nazis decided to eliminate the people they regarded as most dangerous, undesirable, and unneeded—the intelligentsia. The Polish political, cultural, and social elite, along with anyone suspected of organizing a resistance movement, thus became the victims of mass arrests.

Even before entering Polish territory, the Nazis had drawn up special lists of Poles marked for arrest. In November 1939, the Gestapo arrested a large number of professors from institutions of higher education in Cracow and deported them to Sachsenhausen concentration camp. Approximately 12,000 people from the Gdańsk coastal region were murdered at Piaśnica Wielka from September 1939 through April 1940, under an operation to destroy the Polish intelligentsia. The Nazis carried out an operation referred to by the code-name "AB" in the General Government in 1940, arresting several thousand members of the Polish intelligentsia before sending them to the concentration camps or shooting them.

On October 2, 1940, Hitler stated that "all members of the Polish intelligentsia should be wiped out. That sounds harsh, but such is the law of life".[6] SS Reischführer Heinrich Himmler, in charge of all the concentration camps and death camps, said in a similar vein that "the most important task is to unmask all Polish leaders . . . so that they can be neutralized . . . . All expert workers of Polish origins will be utilized in our war industry. Afterwards, all Poles will vanish from the face of the earth".[7]

The wave of terror in occupied Poland, with which nothing in the western European countries could compare, began in September 1939. As time went on, it grew worse. This was a German reaction both to the Polish resistance movement and to the fact that, once the Third Reich attacked the Soviet Union, the supply lines for the Eastern Front ran through Polish territory. The Nazis therefore needed the maximum degree of security, and intensified the already stringent repression apparatus as a consequence.

This is how Governor General Hans Frank characterized his own policies: "In Prague, for instance, they put up large red posters announcing that seven Czechs were shot that day. I said to myself that if I wanted to put up posters announcing every shooting of seven Poles, the Polish forests could not produce the paper needed to print those posters".[8] This boast was, unfortunately, only a mild exaggeration.

The founding of Auschwitz

These intentions and plans by the German occupation regime are connected with the origins of the Auschwitz camp. The SS founded it in the spring of 1940 as a concentration camp, similar to those that already existed in Nazi Germany. The direct reason for its establishment was the fact that the mass arrests of Poles had filled all the existing prisons to overflowing. The German police authorities then suggested that a camp be set up to hold the people who had been arrested.

A special commission began searching for a suitable site. The final choice fell on a prewar barracks complex of 20 buildings located in the outskirts of the small Polish city of Oświęcim. In the first weeks of the occupation, this part of Polish territory was incorporated within the borders of the Third Reich, and the name of Oświęcim changed to "Auschwitz." The camp there was named Konzentrationslager Auschwitz.

On June 14, 1940, the Gestapo sent the first transport of 728 political prisoners there from the prison in Tarnów. They were Poles, and more than a dozen of them were Polish Jews.

The barracks stood on the periphery of the city and it was easy to isolate them from the outside world. They also had convenient road and rail connections with many Polish cities and the nearby border crossing. These factors prompted the Nazis to expand the camp on an enormous scale. In mid-1941, they began sending not only Poles, but also prisoners of other nationalities there from the countries they occupied, including Soviet POWs, Czechs, the French, and Yugoslavians. These transports also contained Jews who had been arrested during various operations aimed at the population of the occupied countries. For instance, lawyers and judges of Jewish origins were sent to the camp as members of the Polish intelligentsia.

A center for the mass extermination of the Jews

While remaining a concentration camp, Auschwitz began to serve a second function in 1942. It became one of the centers of the mass, immediate extermination of the European Jews.

The majority of the Jews deported for mass extermination were deceived. As a rule, the German authorities promised them new places of settlement and jobs. According to the instructions, they were allowed to take along baggage weighing from ten to fifty kilograms. This is why the Jews brought along clothing, foodstuffs, personal accessories, and such basic household elements as bedding, pots and pans, and rugs. They also took along the tools of their trades. Physicians, for example, took medical equipment and medicine.

The deported Jews were forbidden to take along valuables or large amounts of cash. Nevertheless, many of those who still had some possessions attempted to conceal valuables or currency in their clothing or luggage. When the trains arrived at special railroad sidings or unloading platforms, the people had to leave their baggage behind after disembarking.

The Nazis conducted the deportation of Jews to other death camps—Chełmno nad Nerem (Kulmhof), Treblinka, Bełżec, Sobibór, or Majdanek—in a similar way.

Selection

Selections were a specific feature of Auschwitz and Majdanek, and resulted from the fact that both of these camps had double functions, as sites for the immediate extermination of Jews in the gas chambers, and as concentration camps for labor and the gradual elimination of prisoners of various nationalities.

After the deported Jews left the trains at the unloading platforms or "ramps" in Auschwitz, SS physicians conducted selections during which they picked out those of the new arrivals who were capable of labor and useful, for the moment, to the Third Reich's war production. The sick, the elderly, pregnant women, children, and others regarded as useless were, as a rule, led straight to the gas chambers and killed with poison gas. They usually constituted from 70 to 75% of the transport. There were cases in which this proportion was higher. On occasion, an entire newly arrived transport was sent straight to the gas chambers without selection.

A Greek Jew deported to Auschwitz describes the arrival of the transport: "Early in the morning on the fourteenth day of the journey, our train arrived at a station. Many lights were visible through the little window in the freight car. SS men pushed their way into the freight cars with rifles, clubs, and whips in their hands. Shoving us blindly to the left and the right, they screamed '*Raus, alle heraus, schneller, schneller*!!!' People pushed and jostled with all their might towards the exit, swooning with dread.

"Little Mordechai, my baby son, was in my arms all the time. He was half-alive, and had fainted. At a certain moment, I do not know when or how, when the frenzied crowd was pushing towards the exit, my child slipped from my grasp! The enormous wave of people trampling everything broke over me, over my family, over everything, everything! I could not understand anything more, anything. Only the horrible screaming of the Germans could be heard!

"Everything was lost in a single moment. Sylia, the baby—and perhaps me, too! The Germans were screaming. 'Younger ones off to the side, line up, only the young!' They shoved the women, children, old people, the sick, the dead, and the half-dead into trucks. They took them somewhere. We did not know where".[9]

The gas chambers

The Jews classified as unfit for labor were taken to die in the gas chambers. In order to avoid panic and mutiny, the SS usually deceived its victims. They promised them that they would bathe and then be united with their families. It must be borne in mind that the majority of the people were badly exhausted after the long, fatiguing journey, and were dreaming of a shower and something to drink. This explains why, as a rule, they marched towards the gas chambers calmly and without misgivings. Auschwitz commandant Rudolf Höss recalled in his autobiography that whenever the SS caught site of any agitation among the people going to their deaths, "those who were spreading it... were killed with a small-bore rifle in such a way that the others would not notice".[10]

In order to lull the victims and lend credence to what the SS had said, multilingual signs on the doors to the gas chambers announced that they led to disinfection and the showers.

Once the gas chamber was full, the doors were sealed hermetically. SS men protected by gas masks opened cans of Zyklon-B and poured the granules of diatomaceous earth impregnated with hydrogen cyanide into the gas chambers through special openings. The people locked in the chamber were killed by the gas that the granules gave off.

The bodies of the murdered Jews were dragged out of the gas chambers. Their hair was cut off and dental work and jewelry made of precious metals were removed. Then the bodies were burned in the crematorium furnaces or, when the furnaces had insufficient capacity, in the open air.

The number of victims of immediate mass extermination

The Jews who were murdered in the gas chambers immediately after arrival were not entered in the camp records. That is, they were not given numbers and were not registered in the way that this was done with people assigned to labor as prisoners or POWs. The camp authorities attempted to remove the evidence of their crimes and to destroy documents and transport lists bearing the names of the victims. This also makes it extremely difficult to define with precision the number of victims murdered in the gas chamber immediately after arrival. Copies of the transport lists bearing the names of deported Jews have been preserved in some countries, such as France, Holland, and Belgium. No such documentation, however, is extant for the transports of Jews dispatched from the ghettos that had been established in occupied Poland. In such cases, only estimates are possible.

It can be stated on the basis of the existing documentation that the Nazis deported at least 1,100,000 Jews to Auschwitz, although the actual figure was probably higher. The most numerous groups deported to Auschwitz were Jews from Hungary (over 400,000) and from Poland (at least 300,000).

The prisoners of Auschwitz

From the moment of its foundation until January 1945, Auschwitz functioned as a concentration camp where the Nazis imprisoned people of various nationalities. As opposed to the victims of immediate extermination in the gas chambers, these prisoners were scrupulously noted and entered in the camp records. The SS registered and assigned numbers to a total of over 400,000 persons.

The largest group comprised of Jews selected as capable of labor from the mass transports sent to Auschwitz for extermination, and Jewish prisoners in transports sent to the camp along with prisoners of other nationalities. The number of registered Jews in the camp reached approximately 200,000, which amounted to half of the total number of prisoners. The second most numerous group were the Poles, mostly political prisoners, of whom approximately 140,000 (over 35% of the total number of prisoners) were registered in the camp. The third most numerous group were the 21,000 Roma (5%), followed by the 12,000 Soviet POWs. The remaining 25,000 prisoners represented other nationalities.

Criminals, "anti-socials," Jehovah's Witnesses, and homosexuals were also registered in the camp as prisoners. The classification of prisoners did not always correspond to the facts. Some political prisoners were categorized as criminals.

Extermination through starvation, labor, and destructive living conditions

Two contradictory principles governed the way that the camp authorities treated prisoners. On the one hand, they tried to exploit them to the maximum degree as labor, and on the other hand they attempted to wear them down and destroy them as quickly as possible.

Lagerführer (camp director) Karl Fritzsch sometimes delivered a speech informing newly arrived prisoners of what they should expect. "You have not come to a sanatorium, but to a German concentration camp," Fritzsch told them, "and there is only one way out—through the crematorium chimney. Jews have the right to live for two weeks, priests for a month, and the rest for three months".[11]

Adolf Hitler also spoke frankly about the sense of the existence of the concentration camps. "I don't want the camps to be turned into hotels," he said. "Terror is the most effective political weapon. Everyone who learns what is waiting for him in the camp will think long and hard before doing anything against us".[12]

The writer Primo Levi, a former prisoner, describes his first impressions on arrival at the camp. "We realized then for the first time that there were no words in our language to express that contempt, that destruction of human beings. In a single moment, in an access of almost prophetic intuition, the reality of it dawned on us: we had reached the bottom. It was impossible to descend any lower, a more miserable human existence did not exist, and was unthinkable".[13]

Over half of the registered prisoners died in the camp as a result of starvation, brutal terror, punishments and torture, destructive living conditions, disease and epidemics, and, finally, criminal medical experiments. Murderous labor was another reason for the high death rate among the prisoners. This labor was a source of enormous income for both the SS and for many German companies, such as IG Farbenindustrie and the Hermann Göring Werke. Many prisoners lost their lives as an effect of savage treatment, torture, and beatings at the hands of the SS and their auxiliaries, who were mostly German criminal prisoners. Prisoners also died in individual and collective executions. They were shot at the Death Wall and at the places where they labored, hanged at roll-call assemblies, put to death by lethal injection in the camp clinics, and killed in the gas chambers.

New transports arrived at the camp to replace prisoners who had been worked to death or killed.

The criminal Nazi ideology was the reason that Gypsies were sent to the camp. As mentioned above, they constituted the third largest group of victims, after the Jews and the Poles. Gypsies were arrested throughout the Reich and in several occupied countries, and then deported to the concentration camps on orders that Heinrich Himmler, the chief of German police and the SS, issued in December 1942. The greatest numbers of them were sent to Auschwitz and a specially isolated camp, known as the "family camp," was set up for them at Birkenau. Approximately 21,000 men, women, and children filled this camp. With the exception of 2,000 who were transferred to other camps, they all died as a result of exhaustion, starvation, and disease and epidemics—mostly typhus—or in the gas chambers.

The camp bureaucracy

As mentioned above, the camp authorities kept scrupulous records on Auschwitz Concentration Camp prisoners throughout their incarceration, beginning at the moment of their arrival with the assignment of a camp number and the taking of photographs in three standard poses (the tattooing of numbers, usually on the left forearm, was later introduced as well). Detailed personal forms included not only the prisoners' basic identification data, but also descriptions of their physical appearance and information on their religious denominations, their parents, and the reasons for their arrest and deportation to the camp.

Equally meticulous records were kept when prisoners were transferred to new blocks or sent to the penal company. Reports were filed on punishment and telegrams sent out whenever a prisoner escaped. Similarly, when a prisoner died, this fact was noted in the daily report book, in a death certificate, and even in telegrams sent to the next of kin. When death resulted from lethal injection, hanging, shooting, or other "unnatural causes," a fictional cause and even a fictional time and date of decease were entered on the death certificate and in the death book.

A system of code words and concealment of the truth about the people who were killed was developed almost to the point of perfection. The trucks delivering the poisonous Zyklon-B used to kill Jews in the gas chambers were noted in the schedules as carrying material for the "special treatment" or the "resettlement" of the Jews. Prisoners selected in the hospital or during roll call as unfit for further labor, and therefore sentenced to death, were designated in the documents as "*Sonderbehandlung*" (special treatment) or "*Gesondert untergebracht*" (separate disposition). As already mentioned, a fictitious cause of death was entered on the death certificate and in the death book.

The expansion of the camp complex

At the peak of its expansion and functioning, Auschwitz was made up of three parts. The first and oldest part was the original camp (*Stammlager*), later known as Auschwitz I. This is the camp that came into existence in 1940 on the grounds of the prewar barracks, as described above. It originally consisted of 20 buildings, mostly one-story. In order to hold the constantly growing number of prisoners, new blocks were erected and upper stories added to the one-story buildings in 1941-1942 on the orders of the camp administration.

Men, above all political prisoners, were held here throughout the existence of the camp. In 1941-1942, several blocks were fenced off in order to create—at various times—two temporary camps, for Soviet POWs and for women.

Block no. 11 there contained the central camp jail, where prisoners were sent on suspicion of involvement in the resistance movement, planning escapes, maintaining contact with the outside world, or engagement in other conduct regarded by the camp authorities as illicit. Various kinds of punishment, including death by starvation, were inflicted on prisoners in the cellars of Block no. 11. The first experiments in the use of Zyklon-B for killing were also carried out here. The SS carried out the majority of the executions by shooting on the grounds of the Auschwitz I camp, mostly at the Death Wall. Soviet POWs and Jews who arrived in the camp in the first transports were also murdered here in a provisional gas chamber set up in the morgue at the crematorium.

The majority of the offices from which the administration directed and supervised the further expansion of the camp complex were located in the immediate vicinity of Auschwitz I.

The second part of the complex was the Birkenau camp, also known as Auschwitz II. The Nazis began building it in October 1941 in the village of Brzezinka, three kilometers from Oświęcim. They evicted the Polish population and demolished their confiscated dwellings. This was not only the largest camp within the Auschwitz complex, but also the largest one in the whole Nazi camp system, in terms of the area it covered, the number of barracks, and the number of prisoners held at any one time. Above all, however, this is the place where the most people died. The majority of the apparatus for the mass extermination of the Jews was located at Birkenau: four buildings containing gas chambers and furnaces for burning the corpses of the victims (designated crematoria II, III, IV and V), and two provisional gas chambers installed in houses confiscated from Polish civilians (known as bunkers 1 and 2, or as the little white house and the little red house).

In order to improve the efficiency of the mass extermination of the Jews, a railroad spur with a ramp or unloading platform was built in the middle of the Birkenau camp. It ended adjacent to the gas chambers and crematoria.

The Birkenau camp was diverse in character. It was made up of several separate components with varying uses and histories. There were separate camps for women and men of various nationalities, both Jewish and non-Jewish. There were "family camps" for Jews from the Theresienstadt ghetto and for Roma (Gypsies), and transit camps for Jews from Hungary. There were a quarantine camp for newly arrived prisoners, and a camp where the sick were held and where most of the experiments were carried out (the "hospital camp"). A separate sector, known in the camp as "Kanada," was set aside for gathering and sorting the property plundered from the Jews deported to the camp.

The "camp interest zone"

The area administered by the commandant and controlled by the SS men from the Auschwitz garrison extended far beyond the camp perimeter fence. Covering an additional 40 sq. km., it made up the so-called *Interessengebiet des Konzentrationslagers Auschwitz* (Auschwitz Concentration Camp Interest Zone). Its creation followed the eviction in 1940-1941 of the Polish civilians living in the outskirts of Oświęcim and in nearby villages. These people were forced to move to other localities in the Third Reich or the General Government. Some were deported to camps. The Jews who lived here before the war were deported to ghettos.

Some one thousand dwellings were demolished. Other buildings were assigned to officers and non-commissioned officers from the SS camp garrison, some of whom lived here with their entire families. The Germans took over the industrial plants in the zone. They expanded some and liquidated others, replacing them with new factories connected with Third Reich war production. The camp authorities established their infrastructure in the area near the camp, including warehouses, offices, SS barracks, and welfare services for the SS and their families. Here, too, were the railroad sidings and ramps where transports of deportees were unloaded and put through selection.

The Auschwitz sub-camps

From 1942 to 1944, the Nazis set up an additional network of sub-camps. These were usually sited near various German industrial enterprises or agricultural facilities that made use of prisoners as slave labor. A total of almost 50 sub-camps arose.

The camp authorities created the largest sub-camp, called Buna, in the depopulated Polish village of Monowice near Oświęcim, in 1942. Exploiting the labor of prisoners, POWs, and conscript laborers, the leading German company IG Farbenindustrie built the enormous Buna Werke complex to produce synthetic rubber and fuel.

The Buna camp was the third part of the Auschwitz camp. Known later as Auschwitz III Concentration Camp and Monowitz Concentration Camp, it supervised a network of sub-camps at German industrial facilities, mostly in Silesia.

Thousands of starving prisoners, subject to brutal terror, performing backbreaking labor, and sentenced to death, existed in unrelenting danger in all the parts of the camp complex and in the sub-camps.

The resistance movement

Auschwitz became a synonym for crimes against humanity and the collapse of all moral values. It is inscribed in collective consciousness as a symbol of evil, lawlessness, cruelty, and death. Evil indeed dominated, yet there was also a place in the camp for actions opposed to the overwhelming reign of death and the trampling of human dignity. Many prisoners refused to accept the cruel lot meted out to them by the Nazis. They engaged in deeds of self-defense, resisted passively or actively, and even carried on the underground struggle.

Instances of resistance occurred even among the people sent to the gas chambers immediately upon arrival. Women brought in a Jewish transport from the Bergen-Belsen camp mutinied at Crematorium II in Birkenau in October 1943. When one of the Jewish women realized, in the undressing room that was an antechamber to the gas, that death awaited them, she seized SS man Josef Schillinger's pistol and shot him several times, inflicting mortal wounds. She also shot a second SS man. This was a signal to the other women, who threw themselves on the henchmen. The revolt was suppressed, however, and the women murdered.

The forms of the resistance movement

The clandestine struggle by the prisoners in the concentration camp concentrated mainly on saving fellow sufferers from death and counteracting all symptoms of mental breakdown, demoralization, and depravation. At the same time, enormous efforts were made to find a way of documenting and revealing to the world the truth about what was happening in the camp. Prisoner resistance also took the form of military, political, and cultural activity, as well as expressing itself in religious life.

The Polish researcher into prisoner morality, Alicja Glińska, characterizes the goals and tasks of the clandestine struggle in the camp as "informing the world about the crimes being committed in the camp by the Nazis, and informing the prisoners about the international situation; working for the amelioration of the prisoners' existence through means including the organization of a system for the just distribution of food, medicine, and clothing and the placing of people who had not been depraved in functionary posts; counteracting the national, political, and racial antagonisms incited by the camp authorities; preventing mental and moral breakdowns among the prisoners; protecting the lives of outstanding people and political, scientific and cultural figures; and preparing for combat in case the Nazis attempted to liquidate the camp as the front lines approached".[14]

The attitudes of prisoners in the camp

The individual attitudes and behavior of prisoners had an enormous influence on the morale of the camp community. The deed performed by a Polish Franciscan priest from the Niepokolanów community, Father Maksymylian Maria (Rajmund) Kolbe, became a symbol of great devotion, heroism, and resistance. During roll call in the summer of 1941, before the eyes of the whole camp, Kolbe stepped forward from the ranks and asked an SS man to be permitted to take the place of a prisoner who had previously been selected for death by starvation. The SS man agreed. Father Maksymilian Kolbe died in the starvation bunker, receiving a lethal injection at the end. The prisoner whose place he had taken survived. In 1982, the Roman Catholic Church included Father Kolbe among the saints.

The history of Auschwitz Concentration Camp contains many other instances of attitudes by people who exhibited nobility, courage, and spiritual steadfastness in extreme conditions. During his pilgrimage to the site of the camp, Pope John Paul II paid tribute to Father Maksymilian Kolbe, asking "How many similar victories were won here? They were won by people of various faiths and various ideologies—surely not only by those of religious faith."

The French physician Adelaide Hautval had the courage to refuse to cooperate with SS physicians in carrying out criminal experiments on Jewish women. The Polish midwife Stanisława Leszczyńska saved the lives of newborn infants in defiance of the regulations and the will of the SS. The German Otto Küsel used his position as *Arbeitsdienst* in the camp labor office to help save the weak and the exhausted. These were examples for others to follow and they restored faith in humanity.

The organized underground movement

Opposition to the fate that the Nazis prepared for the prisoners was not confined to spontaneous individual deeds. Organized clandestine activity also occurred. The Polish political prisoners who then constituted the decided majority of the camp community took the lead in creating the underground during the first years of Auschwitz Concentration Camp. One of the founders was the Polish Resistance Movement activist Witold Pilecki (known in the camp as Tomasz Serafiński). He went down in history as "the man who volunteered for Auschwitz." He deliberately allowed himself to be arrested during a street roundup in Warsaw in September 1940 in order to reach Auschwitz Concentration Camp and found a clandestine organization there. In 1940-1941, military groups and political socialists and nationalists formed the Polish clandestine movement. Their unification in 1942 gave rise to a strong, homogenous organization that identified with the Home Army (AK) and used that name in the camp. The prisoner who headed it was Col. Juliusz Gilewicz (shot in a collective execution of prisoners on October 11, 1943). The Home Army in the camp was the counterpart of the largest of Polish resistance organizations, which operated under the same name in occupied Poland, and was subordinated to the Polish government-in-exile in London. Leftist groups also functioned in the camp, with the leading role played by members of the Polish Socialist Party (PPS).

Prisoners of other nationalities also carried out resistance work in the camps. Austrian-German, French,

Russian, Jewish, Czech, and Yugoslavian secret groups, leftist in character, arose in the camp in late 1942 and early 1943. In the latter year, they joined some of the Polish socialists and leftists to form a joint international organization called *Kampfgruppe Auschwitz* (Auschwitz Fighting Group). In 1944, the Home Army and the *Kampfgruppe Auschwitz* convened an Auschwitz Military Council, which had the task of preparing an uprising in the camp.

Self-help and prisoner solidarity

Self-help played a special role in the activities aimed at saving prisoners. It consisted of everyday acts of fellowship and mutual aid. At times, it amounted to simple, everyday signs of kindness—a friendly word, a human gesture, a warning against danger, the bandaging of a wound, or giving water to the suffering. It often also took the form of acts that, under camp conditions, required dedication and determination, as, for instance, when prisoners gave up part of their starvation-level food rations for the sake of a friend, shared the contents of the food packages they obtained from home, or took the place of a worn-out fellow prisoner in performing the most arduous labor. There were also more complicated, risky, and dangerous efforts, like stealing food or medicine from the SS warehouses for friends in need, or help in escapes, or hiding the sick from selection for the gas chambers, or falsifying information in the camp records in order to save someone from the threat of death. Benedykt Kautsky, a German of Jewish origin, avoided selection for the gas chamber in just this way. When Kautsky was in the hospital in Monowice (Auschwitz III Concentration Camp) in January 1943, Gustav Herzog, a Jew from Austria who held the important post of report scribe, took the risky and dangerous step of altering the information in Kautsky's camp records to indicate that the latter was a German political prisoner. Wanda Marossanyi and Walentyna Konopka, Polish prisoners assigned to the offices in the Birkenau camp, saved a Jewish Polish woman, Maria Kozakiewicz, the same way. They risked their lives by changing her personal questionnaire to "Aryan," as a result of which she was transferred, as a Polish woman, to a different camp.

Prisoner self-help went hand-in-hand with solidarity, which extended to various spheres. One was the provision of additional food to prisoners who had no source of nutrition aside from the camp rations. Soviet POWs and Jews, to whom food parcels could not be sent, were among the beneficiaries. Prisoners in the Birkenau quarantine camp set a splendid example of solidarity in 1944. They took care of a twelve-year-old Italian boy named Luigi Ferri, risking their lives to hide him in various barracks from the SS men who wanted to kill him. Ferri survived thanks to the help of fellow prisoners. One of his protectors was Otto Wolken, a Jewish physician from Vienna.

The Jewish prisoner Noemi Judkowski reported that Jewish women from Greece and Poland kept the strict Yom Kippur fast and left their bowls full of soup standing at the foot of the wall in a Birkenau barracks. The bowls were still there the following evening. Despite the torments of hunger, no one touched them. A woman named Iza, the room supervisor in the barracks, also expressed solidarity and respect by saying that "We Christian prisoners wish our Jewish sisters the quickest possible return to freedom so that they can observe future holidays with their families".[15]

Solidarity also included such political efforts as combating nationalism, chauvinism, and antisemitism. The goal was to create a united front of prisoner opposition to the SS. Underground organizations in the camp worked in this direction.

The efficacy and extent of self-help and solidarity depended in many instances on the prisoners holding certain functions in the camp, the so-called "prisoner government." The camp underground therefore made repeated efforts to place prisoners of high moral standards in the positions of block supervisor, capo, and assistant capo. Political prisoners sent to the camp for ideological reasons acquitted themselves best in such cases. Efforts were made to remove the criminal prisoners installed by the SS from such positions. This was particularly true of those who showed exceptional savagery and cooperated with the camp authorities in wearing the prisoners down. The principle of the lesser evil was sometimes chosen in dealing removing such perpetrators. So it was in the case of Birkenau "camp senior prisoner" (*Lagerälteste*) Leo Wietschorek, a German political prisoner and a sadist who tormented the prisoners. He was deliberately infected with typhus and died on July 3, 1942. Similar steps were taken against prisoners unmasked as Gestapo informers. The Austrian Hermann Langbein, a member of the *Kampfgruppe Auschwitz* leadership, achieved a great deal both in counteracting the informers and saving other prisoners. Langbein was secretary to SS chief physician Eduard Wirths, and sometimes managed to intercede successfully with Wirths to the benefit of prisoners.

Escapes from the camp

Organizing escapes was an effective means of self-defense and fighting for survival. The greatest opportunities for overcoming the vigilance of the SS guards existed at labor sites outside the camp, and this is where prisoners escaped most frequently. The attitude of local civilians in the area around the camp had enormous significance in determining the success of escapes. In July 1940, the Auschwitz commandant wrote to the supreme SS and police commander in Wrocław that "the local population is fanatically Polish and . . . ready for every chance to act against the hated camp SS garrison. Every prisoner who manages to escape can count on all possible help as soon as he reaches the first Polish farmhouse".[16]

It should be emphasized here that many Poles secretly aided the prisoners. The local civilian population, thinned by evictions, deportation for forced labor in

Germany, arrest, and deportation to the camps, did so spontaneously. Their material situation was dire, and exacerbated by confiscation, compulsory agricultural deliveries, food regulations, and the system of ration cards for foodstuffs that the occupation authorities enforced rigorously. Local underground organizations, mainly the Home Army (AK), Polish Socialist Party (PPS), and Peasant Battalions (BCh), supported by their clandestine regional and central headquarters and by charitable organizations, worked in an organized way for the sake of the prisoners. Poles organized clandestine feeding points for prisoners laboring outside the camp, helped them to correspond with their families, and supplied them with medication and warm clothing. The Polish political prisoner Janusz Pogonowski (hanged in a mass execution in the camp on July 19, 1943) confirmed the receipt of medicine from the local underground in a 1942 secret message, where he wrote: "I obtained approximately 1,000 ampoules of various medications (Coramina, Digipuratuum, Calc. gluc., etc.). All delivered to the infirmary in Au. Conc. C.".[17] In another secret message from later in the autumn of that same year, his compatriot Stanisław Kłodziński informed the Polish underground that most of the medicines used in the camp hospital came from illegal sources. "Official medicines cover 20% of the needs. Yours, approx. 70%. Civilian medicines stolen from the SS infirmary, approx. 10%. It all depends on you, you are the ones".[18]

Thanks to the attitude of Polish civilians, escapees from Auschwitz were not left exclusively to their own resources, plus any possible luck. Members of the local resistance repeatedly organized prisoner escapes, and then concealed the escapees. They conducted them to other, safer regions far from the camp and assured them of shelter there. They also made it possible for escapees to join partisan units. The first escape took place as early as July 6, 1940, at the very beginning of the existence of Auschwitz. The escapee was Tadeusz Wiejowski, who was aided by his fellow Poles who belonged to the resistance movement and were employed in the camp as so-called civilian workers. Wiejowski escaped disguised in work clothes. Five Polish workers were imprisoned in the camp for aiding him. Only one of them survived, and he died shortly after the war. Four Polish prisoners, Kazimierz Piechowski, Stanisław Gustaw Jaster, Józef Lempart and Eugeniusz Bendera, made a bold escape on June 20, 1942. They broke into an SS warehouse and stole uniforms and weapons. Disguised as SS men, they made their way out of the closed, heavily guarded area around the camp in a stolen car. After they reached the General Government, Jaster delivered a secret report drawn up on the camp by Witold Pilecki to Home Army Headquarters.

The escape of the Pole Edward Galiński and the Jew Mala Zimetbaum on June 24, 1944, on the other hand, ended in failure. Disguised as an SS man, he led her through the closed camp zone. They were captured more than ten days later, returned to the camp, and executed after brutal interrogation. A month later, on July 21, the Pole Jerzy Bielecki and the Jew Cyla Cybulska tried the same strategy, this time with success. They both reached the General Government, where Bielecki joined a partisan unit and Cybulska remained in hiding with a Polish family until the end of the war.

Escapees who later wrote reports about the camp and the crimes being committed there by the Nazis were especially significant. *German Extermination Camps – Auschwitz and Birkenau*, published in Washington in November1944, was made up of such reports, by the Pole Jerzy Tabeau and the Jews Rudolf Vrba (known in the camp as Walter Rosenberg), Alfred Wetzler, Arnošt Rosen, and Czesław Mordowicz, who escaped from Auschwitz II-Birkenau. Tabeau escaped from the camp along with another Pole on the night of November 19, 1943. They short-circuited the electrified fence and cut the barbed wire. The SS men in the guard towers opened fire, but the darkness and the rising mist favored the escapees. Vrba and Wetzler escaped early the following April, taking advantage of a hiding place that had been prepared ahead of time in the camp. Rosin and Mordowicz escaped at the end of May in a similar way, but from a different hiding place near Birkenau.

Calculations indicate that 802 prisoners, including 45 women, attempted to escape. Not all the attempts succeeded. Poles (396) were the most numerous escapees, followed by Soviet citizens (179) and Jews (115).

Prisoner mutinies

The prisoner underground reckoned on organizing an armed uprising against the Nazis, and made extensive preparations. The movement in the camp agreed a detailed plan for an uprising with the Polish underground, which was supposed to support the prisoners in the fight against the camp garrison and German units stationed nearby. Despite the advanced state of the preparations, the camp resistance leadership never decided to give the signal for the uprising. The balance of forces was too unequal. The enemy disposed of tremendous firepower and might massacre thousands of people behind barbed wire in revenge.

While the general uprising in the camp never occurred, there were mutinies by some groups of prisoners who found themselves directly under threat. The Polish prisoners in the penal company mounted a combined mutiny and escape while laboring in the drainage ditch in Birkenau on June 10, 1942. Only seven made it out. In reprisal, the SS shot twenty Poles from the penal company and murdered over three hundred others in the gas chamber. Soviet POWs attempted another combined mutiny and escape in Birkenau on November 6, 1942. They took advantage of fog and the falling twilight to push past an SS outpost into a part of the camp that was under construction and not yet fenced off. The majority of them were shot or captured in the subsequent chase. Jews from the *Sonderkommando* launched a dramatic mutiny in Auschwitz II-Birkenau on October 7, 1944. They set one of the crematoria on fire, making it inoperable. Some of them managed to cut the barbed wire and escape from the camp. However, they were surrounded by the pursuing SS and murdered. Approximately 250 Jews died, including the leaders and organizers of the mutiny, Zalmen Gradowski and Józef Deresiński. The SS lost three killed and a dozen or more wounded. In reprisal, the camp authorities massacred 200 prisoners from the *Sonderkommando*. Four Jewish women, including Regina Saferstein, were executed publicly for stealing explosive material from the Union Werke armaments factory and delivering it to members of the *Sonderkommando*.

Collecting records and evidence of crimes

The resistance movement made unceasing efforts to convey the truth about Auschwitz to the world. Prisoners risked their lives to collect information and data on SS crimes, and write them up in the form of notes and reports. They also made copies and took extracts from the Nazi records. They covertly took photographs during extermination operations. At times, they even secretly removed records from the camp offices.

Some materials were concealed on the grounds of Auschwitz Concentration Camp in the hope that they would be discovered someday. These included notes in which members of the *Sonderkommando* provided information on the tragedy and destruction of the Jews, a record book from the Gypsy camp containing some 21,000 names with annotations on deaths, and prints of SS photographs of the progress of camp construction and expansion, including the extermination apparatus. These items were in fact discovered after the war, recovered, and published.

A significant portion of the information, reports, and documents on Nazi crimes (especially on the Holocaust of the Jews and the destruction of Poles, Gypsies, and Soviet POWs), however, was smuggled out to the Polish resistance movement, most frequently in the form of secret messages, while the camp was in operation. Polish prisoners played a leading role in these efforts. They maintained the clandestine contacts with the outside world that made it possible to convey secret correspondence.

Informing the world about Nazi crimes

The Polish resistance movement received secret messages and materials from the camp, and later used them in publications and the underground press, or sent them to the West through the Polish government-in-exile in London. The Polish government then used this material to inform Western public opinion about the crimes at Auschwitz. It did this through publications and the press, including such English-language titles as the *Polish Fortnightly Review*, and also through diplomatic channels. The government also announced and published reports that told the world the truth about Auschwitz, and in particular about the mass extermination of Jews there, and the destruction of Poles. Thanks to these efforts, the world learned the truth about the camp while the war was still going on.

In 1944, the camp resistance movement drew up a "list of henchmen" from Auschwitz. These were the SS men most responsible for the crimes. The Polish underground sent the list secretly to London, and the BBC radio broadcast it to the world, indicating that the criminals on the list had already been sentenced to death by the allies. This caused great unrest among the camp garrison, to the delight of the prisoner population. Józef Cyrankiewicz, a Polish member of the *Kampfgruppe Auschwitz* leadership, reported to the Polish underground in a May 1944 secret message that "they are very frightened by all this commotion. Let me add that the death sentences against 15 SS-führers as announced by London has been making a big impression for some time on those who were sentenced, and some of them have had breakdowns".[19]

The torpedoing by the Allies in the second half of 1944 of the so-called Moll plan was a highly effective step. This was an SS plan to liquidate Auschwitz and murder the prisoners as a way of destroying the evidence of the crimes. Prisoners sent news of this plan to London by way of the Polish resistance movement. The Polish government-in-exile passed the information on to the Allies while asking them to take steps to save the prisoners. The Western Allies responded by issuing a joint declaration that revealed the existence of the Moll plan and threatened that those responsible for such a crime would be held responsible. The declaration and the warning were announced by Radio Washington and the BBC on October 10, 1944. The Allied step proved effective. The SS leadership had to give up on carrying out the plan. This saved the lives of thousands of prisoners, mostly Jewish, who then made up by far the largest group among the camp population.

Spiritual resistance

Resistance to the inhuman system of terror and extermination also extended to the spheres of religion and culture. Faith and covert religious practice often shaped the attitudes and behavior of the prisoners, strengthening their will to survive and their hope of endurance, and bolstering their spirits, reawakening the faith in mankind that had been shaken by camp conditions and helping the prisoners to maintain those values that the Nazis were attempting to destroy. Prayer brought relief and respite. Clandestine observances became a powerful and lasting spiritual experience for prisoners. In a secret message smuggled out of the Death Block and dated August 21, 1944, the Polish prisoner Wacław Stacherski told his wife that "God exists, although it is difficult to believe it today. His will be done. Yesterday, on Sunday, I listened through the cellar window to the mass being said secretly on the ground floor. I took communion later. They lowered the wafer to me on a string".[20] In the notes written during the war by *Sonderkommando* member Zalmen Gradowski and discovered years later, we read: "An initially small, but constantly growing group of people who pray has emerged from the family of 500 believers and nonbelievers, embittered and indifferent. . . . It sometimes happens that comrades who do not pray are also caught up in those sung prayers. . . . They have heard a new sound that awakens and consoles them. . . . A Jew again takes the wings of consolation and believes for certain that tomorrow will be more beautiful than today. . . . He forgets about the present day, and is already living in tomorrow. . . . New hope infuses his blood and strengthens him".[21]

Like religion, so also culture—music and song, literature and poetry, art, education, and learning—frequently became a form of spiritual self-defense and of fighting to maintain humanity. The heritage of camp culture is documentary in nature. It consists above all of portraits of prisoners done in secret and drawings depicting scenes from camp life. Deserving of notice among camp writing is verse expressing the feelings and experience of camp poets while also laying bare and leveling accusations against the inhuman Nazi system.

Other forms of clandestine activity

Clandestine activity in the camp sometimes involved activity that did not bring the prisoner population any real benefits, and yet hampered the Nazis in various ways. These included sabotage committed by the prisoners in German factories, at the experimental growing station for the rubber-bearing kok-sagiz plant in Rajsko near the camp, or in the Zerlegebetrieb labor detail near Birkenau, which dismantled damaged aircraft. Such activity also embraced espionage for the Allies. In a secret message of June 14, 1943, the prisoner Stanisław Kłodziński, who has already been mentioned here, informed the Polish Underground that "an enormous Werk-hall of the Krupp company is being built just near our blocks on the camp terrain. Machinery has been installed recently. I suppose that a month from now it will be time for the birds to fly over. As far as we're concerned, don't feel inhibited, we'll willingly document once again the fact that destroying the enemy is important to us. So don't be inhibited by the fact that we live here. The Krupp company should be destroyed and razed to the ground".[22]

The prisoners' underground struggle in these special and dangerous conditions lasted as long as the camp was in existence, and yielded tangible results. It made it possible to save many prisoners from death. Many of them recovered the faith in mankind and human goodness and altruism that had frequently been endangered in the dreadful camp conditions. Communicating proof of Nazi crimes to the world while the war was still going on represented a big success for the Polish underground. The thousands of documents, reports, and secret messages accumulated by the prisoners are a valuable source of knowledge for researchers into the Auschwitz Concentration Camp.

The Evacuation and Liquidation of the camp

Near the end of 1944, as the Red Army offensive drew near Oświęcim, the camp authorities set about liquidating the evidence of their crimes. The majority of prisoners capable of further labor were evacuated into the depths of the Reich. A few were left behind and not murdered by the SS. Red army soldiers liberated them on January 27, 1945.

Before leaving the camp, the Nazis ordered the dismantling of certain buildings and the demolition of others. For instance, the three crematoria containing gas chambers and furnaces for burning corpses were blown up. They transferred the majority of documents and items plundered from the victims into the depths of Germany, or burned them. Despite these efforts, they did not manage to destroy everything. Many buildings, objects, and documents, as well as personal possessions of the victims, remained. Today they bear witness to the enormity of the crimes committed here.

The founding of the Auschwitz-Birkenau Museum

Several months after the end of the war and the liberation of the Nazi camps, a group of Polish prisoners who had managed to survive the hell of Auschwitz began propagating the idea of commemorating the victims of the largest death camp. As early as December 1945, former prisoner Alfred Fiderkiewicz presented it publicly during a session of the provisional Polish parliament, the People's National Council in Warsaw. In April 1946, a group of Polish survivors arrived at the site of the camp with the intention of opening a museum. They looked after the thousands of pilgrims and visitors who had begun coming on a mass scale to search for some trace of relatives, to pray for them, and to pay homage to those who had been murdered.

On July 2, 1947 the Polish *sejm* passed a law securing the grounds and buildings at the Auschwitz site as a place of international martyrdom and calling into being the Oświęcim-Brzezinka State Museum for this purpose.

The task of the Museum, as fixed by the law, was to secure the grounds and buildings of the camp, and to collect and gather together evidence and material related to the Nazi crimes so that they could be studied and made accessible to the public.

The newly created Museum included the two extant parts of the camp complex, the so-called main camp (Auschwitz I) in Oświęcim and the Birkenau camp (Auschwitz II) in Brzezinka. The Museum thus included the places where the camp authorities had installed almost all the apparatus of mass extermination, as well as the majority of the buildings, blocks, and barracks where the prisoners were housed. However, many other sites and buildings connected with the functioning of Auschwitz Concentration Camp lay outside the boundaries of the Museum. Some of these sites, such as some of the sub-camps, were located scores or even hundreds of kilometers from Oświęcim.

In the end, the Museum assumed responsibility for an area of 191 hectares, of which the Memorial at the Auschwitz I site accounted for twenty hectares and the

Memorial at the Auschwitz II-Birkenau site for 171 hectares (including 20 hectares of woods).

There are 154 original camp buildings of various sorts in the Museum and Memorial (56 at Auschwitz I and 98 at Birkenau). These include prisoner blocks and barracks, administration buildings, SS guardhouses, guard towers, and the camp gates. There are also 300 ruins including the ruins of the gas chambers and crematoria; and 13,844 meters of camp fence (2,080 meters at Auschwitz I and 11,764 meters at Birkenau), 10,955 meters of paved roads (2,595 meters at Auschwitz I and 8,360 meters at Birkenau), and 2,200 meters of train tracks.

Thousands of objects belonging to the people who had been doomed to die were found at the site of the camp or nearby after liberation, including suitcases (frequently bearing the names and addresses of their owners), Jewish prayer garments, artificial limbs, glasses, shoes, and human hair. These objects make up a basic part of the Museum holdings. They include approximately 40 m^3 of shoes, 1,950 kg. of human hair, and 40 m^3 of cutlery. There are also 3,500 suitcases, 36,000 pots and pans, and a great many other smaller items, including umbrellas, combs, shaving brushes, toothbrushes, and so on.

The Museum collections also include 6,000 exhibits, including 2,000 works of art done (often illegally) in the camp by prisoners, as well as other works dating from after the war. The Archives contain a vast collection of Nazi documents, as well as material from the prisoner resistance movement, postwar accounts, memoirs, depositions, films, and so on.

The maintenance and preservation of the Auschwitz Memorial

The work of the Museum, the maintenance of the grounds and the conservation of the buildings have been and continue to be the subject of lively discussion among former prisoners, specialists in various fields, and the media. There have been widely divergent voices. Some felt that the site should have been plowed up, removing all traces of genocide, and that a large monument should then have been erected. Others felt that no preservation work should have been carried out and that whatever remained of the camp should have been left to "grow old and perish in dignity." There were, finally, a great many who felt that the site should be preserved to the maximum possible extent and that everything capable of being preserved should be saved for posterity.

In a situation involving such varied conceptions as to the policy of maintaining the site, it has not been easy to carry out preservation work. The technical state of the buildings, and especially the wooden barracks in Birkenau, constructed out of impermanent material, left a great deal to be desired. Other buildings, such as the majority of the apparatus of mass extermination, remained in the form of ruins.

Planned preservation work began in 1955 and continues to this day. Progress depended, and still depends, on the available financial resources. Until the early 1990s, funding for the preservation and maintenance of the Memorial came exclusively from the Polish government. There was no aid from outside Poland, despite the fact that the site was inscribed on the UNESCO World Heritage List in 1979. Only since the 1990s have the Polish efforts been backed by significant funds from other countries. The aid was organized by the Ronald S. Lauder Foundation, whose president took an active role in raising funds for preservation. Thanks to this aid, many essential preservation projects have been completed and important original camp objects saved from destruction in recent years.

In its preservation work, the Museum now follows the principle of interfering as little as possible with the remains of the camp. There has been a radical turning away from the practices of the first period after liberation, when several reconstruction projects were carried out. Professor Bohdan Rymaszewski, chairman of the Preservation Commission of the Auschwitz-Birkenau State Museum International Council, has emphasized that "the general guideline for preservation should be the preservation of today's state as given."

The Museum as a place of education and commemorating the victims

Aside from preservation work, the Museum carries out scholarly research, organizes exhibitions shown in Poland and other countries, issues its own publications, organizes lectures, conferences, seminars, and symposia for teachers and students from Poland and other countries, and offers a year-long postgraduate course for Polish teachers on Totalitarianism, Nazism, and the Holocaust.

The most popular education work is carried out among visitors to the Museum. An average of half a million people come here each year. Through the end of 2002, some 26,000,000 people had visited the site of the camp. Poles made up the decided majority (over 18,000,000), with school students being the most numerous. Increasing numbers of people are also coming from other countries, particularly the USA, Germany, England, Italy, Israel, and France. The visitors sometimes include former prisoners of Auschwitz or other concentration camps who share their recollections of what they experienced.

The Museum attempts not only to present historical events, but above all to perpetuate remembrance of the victims of the camp, showing them not only as statistics, but as real, individual people who were deported here and, for the most part, died.

One form of perpetuating the remembrance of the victims is the meetings held on the occasion of anniversaries, such as that of the liberation of the camp. Former prisoners and their families, government officials, the diplomatic corps, and the media attend. The annual March of the Living is a special form of commemorating the victims: young Jewish people leave hundreds of little plaques bearing the names of holocaust victims at the Birkenau site. On All Souls' Day each year, Oświęcim residents and relatives of the victims go to the site of the camp to light candles and leave flowers. Catholic pilgrims come to the places where saints and the beatified were martyred in the camp.

The grounds and buildings of the two camps, Auschwitz I and Birkenau, are accessible in their totality to visitors. Places associated with specific events in the history of the camp have been explicated and marked by the Museum using a uniform system of black granite tablets bearing texts and photographs taken while the camp was in operation. These markers help make it possible to understand what actually happened at various places, some of which are now only ruins. Ground containing human remains, the ruins of the gas chambers and crematoria, sites of prisoner mutinies and executions, and the buildings where criminal experiments were conducted are all explained, and also commemorated, in this way. An effort has also been made to show who the people sent to their deaths by the Nazis were. In several places, there are tablets bearing photographs of Jews disembarking from the train cars at the unloading ramp, unaware of the threat hanging over them—which is why they are still full of hope. Later photographs show them waiting for selection by SS physicians, and then being led to their deaths in the gas chambers.

Several of the prisoner buildings at the Auschwitz I site contain a general exhibition and the so-called national exhibitions. The general exhibition displays such original objects discovered after the liberation of the camp as victims' suitcases, shoes, artificial limbs, clothing, fringed garments, bowls, pots and pans, the hair shorn from the heads of the people who had been murdered, and the tailor's haircloth into which it was made. The national exhibitions arose on the initiative of former prisoners associated with the International Auschwitz Committee. They illustrate the fate of the citizens of different countries who were deported in transports to Auschwitz.

The Museum attempts to maintain the site of the Birkenau camp in as inviolate a state as possible. Aside from the concise information on the black tablets, there are no contemporary exhibitions or interior arrangements here. The only large added element is the International Monument unveiled in 1967 at the end of the railroad spur among the ruins of the gas chambers and crematoria.

In 2001, work was completed on the preservation and opening to visitors of the largest so-called camp Sauna building in Birkenau. This is the place where newly arrived prisoners were registered, where free human beings went through the process of being transformed into camp numbers without names, hair, or civilian clothing. Prisoners were disinfected here; so was the clothing plundered from the murdered Jews, before it was shipped into the depths of the Third Reich.

A special place in the Sauna is the Wall of Remembrance with the family photographs of Polish Jews from Będzin and Sosnowiec. Discovered after liberation, these snapshots present the everyday, normal life of these people before the Holocaust, and are a reminder and commemoration of the world that the Nazis irrevocably destroyed.

Teresa and Henryk Świebocki

1. *Das Urteil von Nürnberg 1946. DTV Dokumente.* München 1961, p. 44, Nuremberg doc. 386-PS.
2. Gottfried Feder, *Das Program der NSDAP und seine weltanschaulichen Grundgedanken.* München 1932, p. 19.
3. Tomasz Sobański, *Fluchtwege aus Auschwitz.* Warsaw 1980, pp. 5-6, Nuremberg doc. L-003 (Einleitung: Jan Zaborowski).
4. *Das Urteil von Nürnberg*... p. 111, Nuremberg doc. 2915-PS.
5. Hans-Joachim Döring, *Die Zigeuner im nationalsozialistischen Staat.* Hamburg 1964, p. 143 (October 13, 1942 letter from Otto Thierack to Martin Bormann).
6. *Deutsche Politik in Polen 1939-1945. Aus dem Diensttagebuch von Hans Frank, Generalgouverner in Polen.* Immanuel Geiss, Wolfgang Jacobmeyer (Hrsg.), Opladen 1980, pp. 14-15.
7. Karol Maria Pospieszalski, *Polska pod niemieckim prawem 1939-1945.* (in:) Ziemie Zachodnie. Poznań 1946, p. 28 (Abschrift einer Rede Himmlers in deutscher Fassung).
8. *Deutsche Politik in Polen 1939-1945...*, p. 38 (interview with Völkischer Beobachter correspondent Kleiss, November 6, 1940).
9. Halina Birenbaum, *Wołanie o pamięć*, Oświęcim 2000, p. 159.

10. *Auschwitz in den Augen der SS. Rudolf Höß, Pery Broad, Johann Paul Kremer.* Katowice 1981, pp. 93-94 (Aufzeichnungen Rudolf Höß).
11. Archives of the Auschwitz-Birkenau State Museum in Oświęcim (hereafter: ABSM), Resistance Movement Materials (hereafter: RMM), vol. VII, p. 464.
12. Hermann Rauschning, *Gespräche mit Hitler.* Zürich-Wien-New York 1940, pp. 210 ff.
13. Primo Levi, *Czy to jest człowiek?* Auschwitz-Birkenau State Museum in Oświęcim, Książka i Wiedza 1996, p. 28.
14. Alicja Glińska, "Moralność więźniów Oświęcimia." *Etyka* 1967 vol. II, pp. 209.
15. Noemi Judkowski, "U nas w Auschwitz", *Zeszyty Oświęcimskie* 21 (1995), p. 263.
16. Archives of ABSM, D-Aul/13. Documents on the escape of Tadeusz Wiejowskieg, p. 25 (letter of July 19, 1940 from Rudolf Höß to Erich von dem Bach-Zelewski).
17. Archives of ABSM, RMM vol. I p. 5, secret message of August 31, 1942 by Janusz Pogonowski (known in the camp as Skrzetuski).
18. Archives of ABSM, RMM vol. I, p. 12, secret message of November 12, 1942 by Stanisław Kłodziński.
19. Archives of ABSM, RMM vol. II, p. 75, secret message of Józef Cyrankiewicz.
20. Archives of ABSM, RMM vol. XXIX, p. 109, secret message from Wacław Stacherski to his wife.
21. Archives of ABSM, Memoirs Collection, vol. 174, pp. 125-128, manuscript of Załmen Gradowski (translated from Yiddish).
22. Archives of ABSM, RMM, vol. I, p. 32, secret message of Stanisław Kłodziński.

From the editors

We offer our readers this album about Auschwitz Concentration Camp, which contains both archival material from the years when the camp was in operation and contemporary photographs of what is left.

The archival material, in the form of documents and photographs, comes mainly from the collections of the Auschwitz-Birkenau State Museum in Oświęicm, which assumed responsibility after the war for preserving the evidence of Nazi crimes and commemorating the martyrdom and death of the victims. The archival material illustrates the site of the camp and the buildings there in the years 1940-1945 and, more importantly, depicts the fate of the people deported to Auschwitz—both those who were put to death in the gas chambers immediately after arrival, and those who were sentenced to labor and death in the concentration camp.

The contemporary photographs are the work of Adam Bujak, an artist who has held a place among the leading Polish photographers for years. His photographs reflect the present appearance of the site of the concentration camp within the boundaries of the Museum. They depict what is left of the camp, sometimes in its original state and sometimes in the form of ruins, the witness to and evidence of the crimes of an inhuman totalitarian system. These photographs portray the most important things that distinguish the Museum from other similar institutions around the world: the original site of the greatest crime of the twentieth century, the Holocaust. "Soil where the dead are most present," as the sculptor Henry Moore defined the Auschwitz site.

The visual material in the album is supplemented by passages from texts written clandestinely, mostly by prisoners in Auschwitz. Some of them had been buried on the grounds of the camp and were discovered after the war; others were smuggled out of the camp, in the form of secret messages or reports, while the war was still going on. Other texts are passages from accounts, reports, or memoirs that prisoners wrote after escaping from the camp. There are also descriptions of scenes and events that only the perpetrators, the SS men from the camp garrison, could know about and report on. These accounts date from immediately after the war, when the writers were in internment camps or in prison.

It is our most profound hope that the reading of this album will help perpetuate knowledge and the memory of the millions of victims of the Nazi "new order."

May each of us, regardless of our place in society, make the effort to do something so that the world becomes a place where people can live in peace, respecting and accepting others.

The camp was always of interest to the highest levels of the German leadership. This photograph shows the Reichsführer SS during one of his inspections. The photograph was taken in 1942 at a site adjacent to the IG Farbenindustrie synthetic rubber and gasoline plants.

Auschwitz Concentration Camp prisoners built the IG Farbenindustrie complex and then labored there. This photograph was taken during an inspection of the plant in 1942. Himmler, at left; plant director Dr. Faust, middle; Auschwitz commandant Höß, next to Faust.

Auschwitz. The camp garrison, several thousand strong, was made up of members of the elite SS Totenkopfverbände (Death's Head units), specially trained for concentration-camp service (SS photograph from the period when the camp was in operation).

Auschwitz I. The camp gate, with the cynical inscription "Work makes you free," led to the first, oldest part of the camp, known as the Main Camp (*Stammlager*). It was founded in 1940 on the site of prewar Polish barracks that the SS adapted as a camp and surrounded with an electrified fence. Each morning, the labor details marched out through the gate for long hours of backbreaking labor at sites near the camp. Despite the slogan on the gate, labor was one of the methods for breaking down the people sent to the camp, and was never a means for them to attain freedom.

Auschwitz II – Birkenau. The main SS guard tower, which was also the gate that the prisoners called "the Gate of Death," leading to the second and largest part of the Auschwitz camp. The camp authorities began building this camp in 1941. Most of the apparatus for the mass extermination of the Jews was located in this part of the camp—the gas chambers and crematoria in which approximately one million Jews were murdered. Over three hundred single-story barracks were also constructed here to house the prisoners assigned to labor.

Konzentrationslager Auschwitz Art der Haft: Sch. P. Gefg. Nr.: ~~38062~~ 11437 Pol. 39306

Name und Vorname: Polomski, Kasimir

geb.: 25.2.1907 zu: Pabianice, Kr. Lask 60

Wohnort: Niechcice, Post Gorzkowice, Kr. Petrikau, Distr. Radom

Beruf: Lehrer Rel.: r.k.

Staatsangehörigkeit: ehem. Polen Stand: vern.

Name der Eltern: Jozef u. Jozefa geb. Marynowski Rasse: ar.

Wohnort: Pabianice, Robert Kochstr. Nr. 35, Kr. Lask, Wartheland Vater gestorben

Name der Ehefrau: Teodozja geb. Jadwiszczak Rasse:

Wohnort: Niechcice, w.o.

Kinder: keine Alleiniger Ernährer der Familie oder der Eltern: ja

Vorbildung: 4. Kl. p. Volkssch., 8 Kl. Gymn, 2 J. Semin.

Militärdienstzeit: 28 Inf. Regt in Litzmannstadt von—bis 1929-1930

Kriegsdienstzeit: keine von—bis:

Grösse: 1,70 Nase: geradl. Haare: blond Gestalt: kräftig

Mund: dicke Lippen Bart: keinen Gesicht: oval Ohren: norm.

Sprache: poln. Augen: braun-grau Zähne: 5 fehlen

Ansteckende Krankheit oder Gebrechen: keine

Besondere Kennzeichen: keine

Rentenempfänger: nein

Verhaftet am: 4.6.1942 wo: in Niechcice

1. Mal eingeliefert: 6.6.1942 2. Mal eingeliefert:

Einweisende Dienststelle: SD. Radom

Grund: Verdacht der Zugehörigkeit und Betätigung in einer ill. GO.

Parteizugehörigkeit: keine von—bis

Welche Funktionen: keine

Mitglied v. Unterorganisationen: nein

Kriminelle Vorstrafen: ang. keine

Politische Vorstrafen: ang. keine I.T.S. FOL: 1164

Ich bin darauf hingewiesen worden, dass meine Bestrafung wegen intellektueller Urkundenfälschung erfolgt, wenn sich die obigen Angaben als falsch erweisen sollten.

v. g. u. Der Lagerkommendant KL.-Au. i. A.

Polomski Kazimierz 25. II. 1907 r.

The camp was founded for Polish political prisoners, who were brought here from June 14, 1940, through the end of 1944.

Other Poles sent to the camp included people arrested in street roundups, residents of the Zamość region whose land and homesteads were given to German farmers, civilians deported from Warsaw after the start of the Uprising there on August 1, 1944, and professors, priests, political leaders, and other members of the intelligentsia. Polish Jews, including lawyers, physicians, and rabbis, also arrived in the Polish transports.

Häftlings-Personal-Karte

Fam.-Name: Kwiecień

Vorname: Franz

Geb. am: 26.8.1917 in Litzmannstadt

Stand: led. Kinder: -•-

Wohnort: Litzmannstadt

Strasse: Diestelgasse 71

Religion: r.k. Staatsang.: eh. Polen

Wohnort d. Angehörigen: Eltern: Thomas u. Eva geb. Pianowski Adr. wie oben

Eingewiesen am: 11.2.1943

durch: Stapo Litzmannstadt

in KL.: 8.4.43 Au / 14.4.43 Gu.

Grund: Lebensmittelschmuggel nach d. Judenghetto

Vorstrafen:

Überstellt am: an KL.

Entlassung: am: durch KL.: mit Verfügung v.:

Strafen im Lager: Grund: Art: Bemerkung:

HOLLERITH ERFASST

Personen-Beschreibung: Grösse: 168 Gestalt: stark Gesicht: längl. Augen: blau Nase: wellig Mund: normal Ohren: gross Zähne: 4 fehlt Haare: blond Sprache: poln.

Bes. Kennzeichen: Charak.-Eigenschaften: Sicherheit b. Einsatz: Körperliche Verfassung:

The fragmentary extant German records indicate reasons for imprisonment in Auschwitz, such as participation in the resistance movement, aiding Jews, smuggling food into the ghetto, listening to the radio, etc.

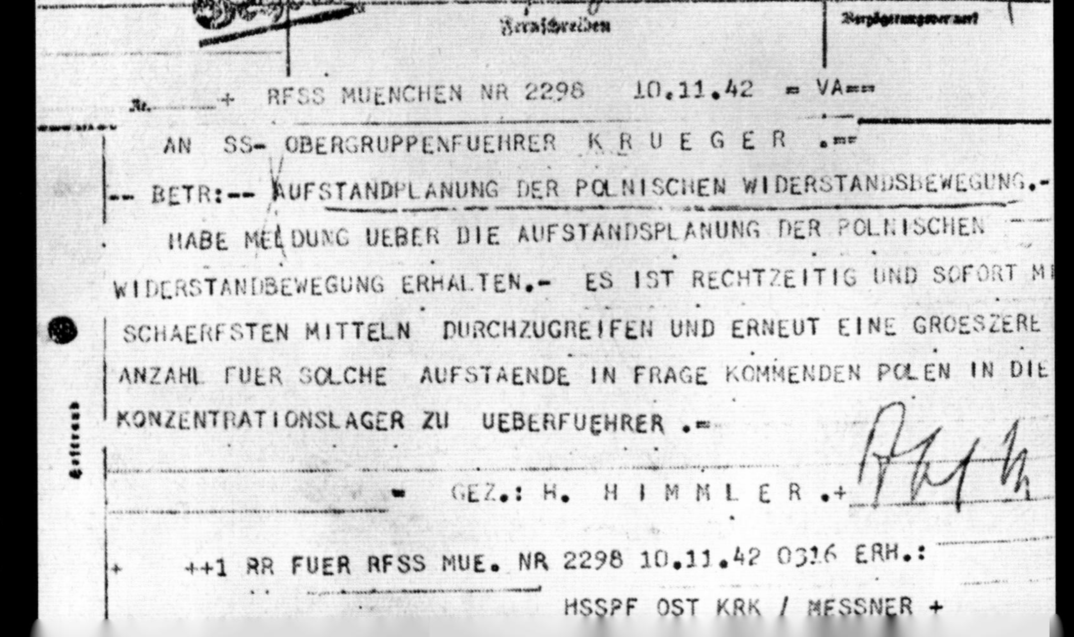

Geheim! Fernschreiben

+ RFSS MUENCHEN NR 2298 10.11.42 = VA==

AN SS- OBERGRUPPENFUEHRER K R U E G E R .==

-- BETR: -- AUFSTANDPLANUNG DER POLNISCHEN WIDERSTANDSBEWEGUNG.-

HABE MELDUNG UEBER DIE AUFSTANDSPLANUNG DER POLNISCHEN WIDERSTANDBEWEGUNG ERHALTEN.- ES IST RECHTZEITIG UND SOFORT M[IT] SCHAERFSTEN MITTELN DURCHZUGREIFEN UND ERNEUT EINE GROESZERE ANZAHL FUER SOLCHE AUFSTAENDE IN FRAGE KOMMENDEN POLEN IN DIE KONZENTRATIONSLAGER ZU UEBERFUEHREN .=

GEZ.: H. H I M M L E R .+

++1 RR FUER RFSS MUE. NR 2298 10.11.42 0316 ERH.:

HSSPF OST KRK / MESSNER +

A telegram signed by the Reichsführer SS, Heinrich Himmler, concerning plans to arrest members of the Polish resistance movement and send them to the concentration camps.

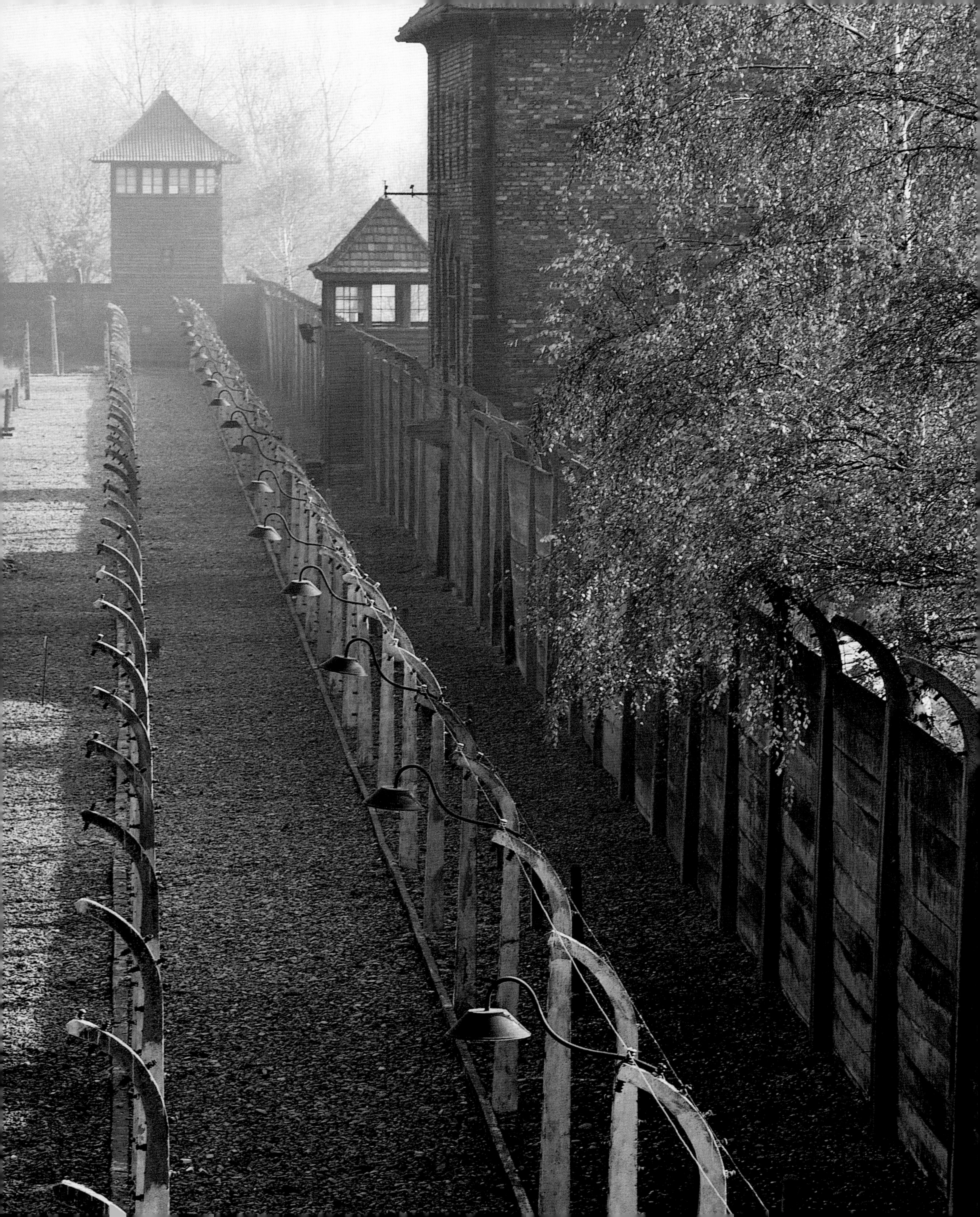

From the memoirs of the Auschwitz Concentration Camp commandant, SS-Obersturmbannführer Rudolf Höß:

"In the summer of 1941 —I cannot give the exact date at this moment —I suddenly received a summons to the Reichsfürer SS in Berlin, which came straight from his adjutant's office. Uncharacteristically, Himmler informed me without the presence of his adjutant of the following:
'The Führer has ordered the final solution of the Jewish question. We, the SS, are to carry out the order. The existing extermination sites in the east cannot cope with the large scale of the planned operation. I have therefore designated Auschwitz for this purpose, both in view of its favorable location from the transport point of view, and because that area can easily be isolated and camouflaged. At the beginning, I intended to entrust this task to one of the higher SS officers, but decided against doing so because I wanted to avoid from the outset any difficulties in the limitation of authority. I am therefore now entrusting you with this task. This is difficult, demanding work that requires...

...total dedication regardless of whatever problems crop up. You will learn the details from Sturmbannführer Eichmann of the RSHA, who will report to you in the immediate future. The departments involved will be notified by me at the appropriate time.
'You are to keep this order in strict secrecy, even from your superiors. After the discussion with Eichmann you will send me ...

Protocol of the January 20, 1942 conference at Berlin-Wannsee. High Third Reich officials including the chief of the Sicherheitspolizei, Reinhard Heydrich, and Adolf Eichmann of the Reichssicherheitshauptamt (RSHA) took the executive decisions for conducting the "Final Solution of the Jewish Question"—in other words, the mass extermination of the Jews. Page 6 of the document contains a precise calculation of the number of Jews scheduled for extermination, with a breakdown of the specific regions involved. The overwhelming majority, over 80% of them, lived in the eastern part of Europe.

Land	Zahl
A. Altreich	131.800
Ostmark	43.700
Ostgebiete	420.000
Generalgouvernement	2.284.000
Bialystok	400.000
Protektorat Böhmen und Mähren	74.200
Estland - judenfrei -	
Lettland	3.500
Litauen	34.000
Belgien	43.000
Dänemark	5.600
Frankreich / Besetztes Gebiet	165.000
Unbesetztes Gebiet	700.000
Griechenland	69.600
Niederlande	160.800
Norwegen	1.300
B. Bulgarien	48.000
England	330.000
Finnland	2.300
Irland	4.000
Italien einschl. Sardinien	58.000
Albanien	200
Kroatien	40.000
Portugal	3.000
Rumänien einschl. Bessarabien	342.000
Schweden	8.000
Schweiz	18.000
Serbien	10.000
Slowakei	88.000
Spanien	6.000
Türkei (europ. Teil)	55.500
Ungarn	742.800
UdSSR	5.000.000
Ukraine 2.994.684	
Weißrußland ausschl. Bialystok 446.484	
Zusammen: über	11.000.000

...the blueprints for the planned apparatus immediately. The Jews are the eternal enemy of the German people and must be eradicated. All Jews who fall into our hands will be annihilated during the course of this war, without exception . . . '"

Auschwitz I. The SS converted
a prewar ammunition bunker into
Crematorium I in the summer of 1940.
They used it to burn the corpses of
people who had died in the camp
as a result of starvation or being
worked to death, or who had been
shot or died in other ways. The first
operations for the mass murder
of Jews were carried out in early 1942
in the morgue of Crematorium I,
which was adapted as a gas chamber.

Auschwitz II – Birkenau. View of the camp from the main SS guardhouse. The Germans built a railroad spur here and used it for trains carrying deportees.

Part of Sector B II in the Birkenau camp. The camp was divided into six separate parts, each of which was an autonomous camp, numbered from B IIa to B IIf. The fifth sector, B IIe, was assigned to the Gypsies. Thirty-two wooden barracks were built there. These were German field stables, adapted for camp use. Several hundred prisoners were crowded into each barracks. The camp for Gypsies was located here from February 26, 1943 to August 2, 1944, when the SS put the last surviving Gypsies, approximately 3,000 people, to death in the gas chambers.

The Gypsy Book is an exceptional, one-of-a-kind document concerned in its entirety with a single ethnic group. It contains some 21,000 entries with the names and other identifying information on the Gypsy families imprisoned in the so-called family camp at Birkenau in 1943. The majority of the Gypsies died in the camp as a result of disease and typhus epidemics and starvation, or in the gas chambers. The book was stolen by Polish prisoners assigned to register the Gypsies, and buried in a bucket on the Birkenau grounds.

Pages from the death book for Soviet prisoners of war, containing their camp numbers, first and last names, and the day and time they died, along with fictitious causes of death.

From a secret message sent by a Polish political prisoner: "From the beginning, the treatment of them showed that no one here...

...even thought of observing the regulations of international law covering POWs. Marched naked to de-lousing, they were marched naked to the blocks—they were partially clothed in overalls, and the lucky ones got shoes. . . . Beaten, without a moment's respite, half-naked, freezing, weak . . . Death gathered its harvest."

A transport of Soviet POWs. Photograph taken during the war.

Auschwitz II – Birkenau. The oldest part of the Birkenau camp was located in sector B I. At first, the only buildings here were brick barracks. POWs worked on their construction. Bricks from the farmsteads whose Polish owners had been evicted were used. When they ran out of bricks, the camp authorities adapted German field stables for use as barracks for prisoners.

Auschwitz II – Birkenau.
Part of the camp.

Prisoners of various nationalities were sent to the concentration camp. They were scrupulously registered and assigned numbers in place of their names. Until 1943, most of the prisoners were photographed in three poses. The pictures were marked with camp numbers, an abbreviation for the name of the camp (KL), and letters indicating the prisoner's nationality and category—the reason they had been sent to the camp. Most of the prisoners were photographed after having their heads shaved. They were already dressed in striped camp uniforms with their numbers sewn on and a triangle indicating the reason for their arrest. Those classed as political prisoners and held under so-called protective custody (*Schutzhaft*), for instance, wore red triangles. This category included prisoners arrested for actual resistance to the occupation regime, but it also included Poles arrested in street roundups and those deported from the Zamość region where Germans were to be settled. Some Jews were also designated political prisoners, resulting in a star made of two triangles, yellow and red.

Newly arrived Jews after going through the concentration camp "reception procedure": the shaving of their heads, disinfection, and registration.

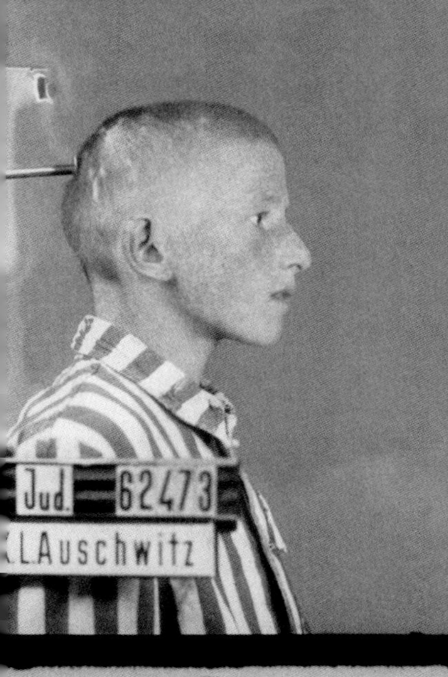
Jud. 62473
K.L.Auschwitz

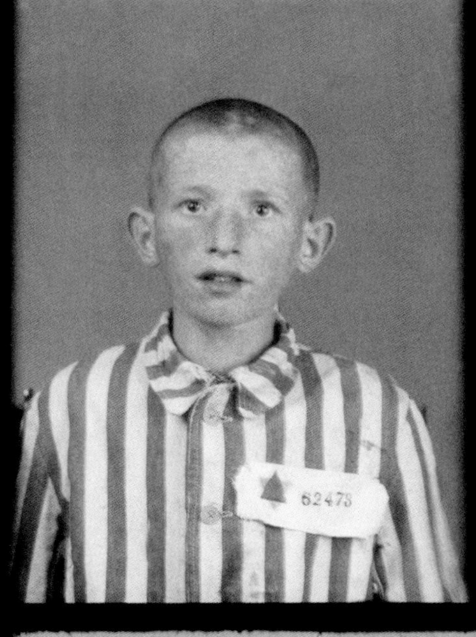
62473

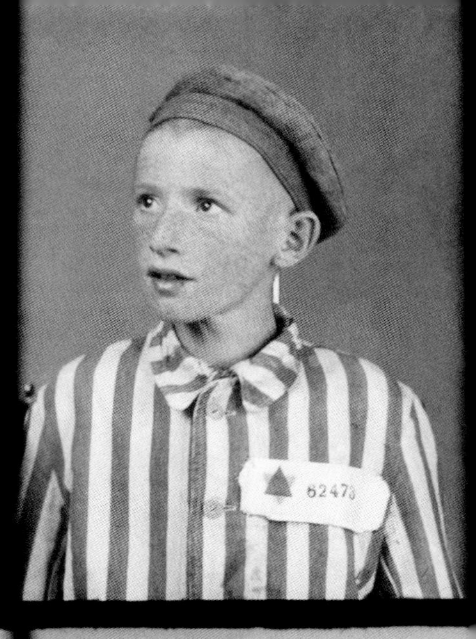
62473

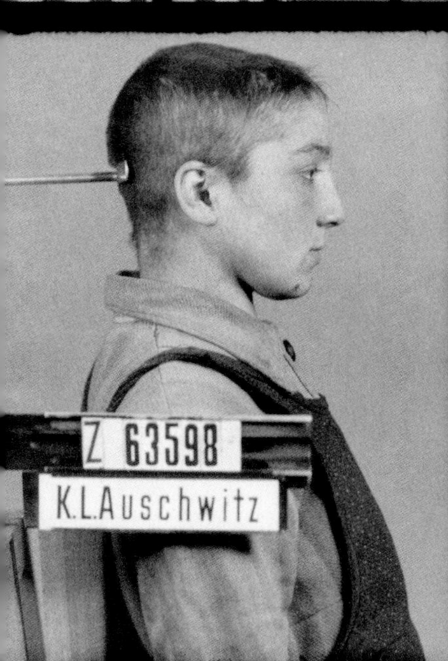
Z 63598
K.L.Auschwitz

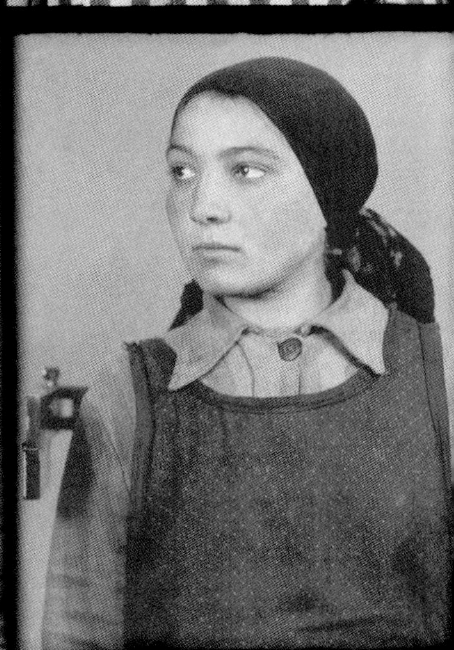

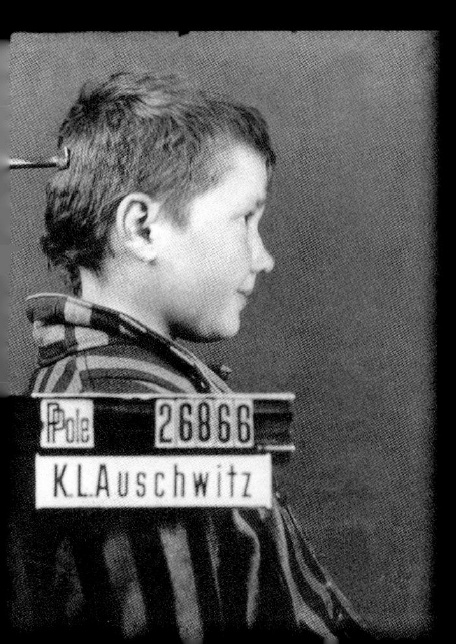
Pole 26866
K.L.Auschwitz

Auschwitz I.
The camp gate and the double barbed-wire fence, which was electrified.

Auschwitz II – Birkenau. Panorama of the camp from the main SS guardhouse, known as the Gate of Death.

Auschwitz I. The camp fence and a guard tower.

VORSICHT
Hochspannung
Lebensgefahr

At left:
One of the signs reading "Caution: high tension. Mortal danger," which surrounded the camp. Entering the zone near the fence was forbidden and caused an instantaneous reaction, in the form of rifle fire, from the SS men in the guard tower. Prisoners sometimes attempted to commit suicide by throwing themselves on the electrified fence.

Letter of May 5, 1943 from the German Security Police and Security Service commander for occupied Holland. It deals with the "solution of the Jewish question" in Holland and the deportation of Jews to the East, to Auschwitz.

Der Befehlshaber
icherheitspolizei und des SD
ie besetzten niederl.Gebiete

B 4 -

Den Haag, den 5.5.1943

G E H E I M !

Betrifft: Endlösung der Judenfrage in den Niederlanden.

Verteiler: An die Zentralstelle für jüdische Auswanderung, Amsterdam (2 Exemplare)
Lager Westerbork
KL. Hertogenbosch
sämtliche Aussenstellen

Auf Grund der letzten Anweisung von ᛋᛋ-Gruppenführer R a u t e und der mit dem Vertreter des RSHA. geführten Besprechungen sollen in der Judenbearbeitung der nächsten Monate folgende Aktionen durchgeführt werden:

1.) Allgemeine Linie:
Der RFᛋᛋ wünscht, dass in diesem Jahre an Juden nach dem Osten abtransportiert wird, was menschenmöglich ist.

2.) Nächste Züge nach dem Osten:
Da in Auschwitz ein neues Bunawerk aufgebaut werden soll, das im Westen durch Luftangriff zerstört wurde, wird vor allem im Monat Mai und Juni eine Höchstzahl von Juden aus dem Westen benötigt. Es wurde vereinbart, dass zunächst die für den Abtransport bereitgestellten Juden durch Zusammenlegung mehrerer Züge möglichst bereits in der ersten Monatshälfte abbefördert werden, also das Lager Westerbork beschleunigt geleert wird. Anzustreben ist für den Monat Mai die Ziffer 8.000. Zugvereinbarungen werden vom BdS. Den Haag mit dem RSHA. getroffen.

3.) Lager Hertogenbosch:
Da das RSHA im Juni weitere 15.000 Juden anfordert, muss möglichst schnell der Zeitpunkt erreicht werden, an dem auch die Insassen des Lager Hertogenbosch beansprucht werden können.

4.) Amsterdam:
Dieses Ziel deckt sich mit der Absicht des Gruppenführers, nach Niederschlagung des gegenwärtigen politischen Widerstandes eine Judenräumungsanordnung für die Stadt Amsterdam zu erlassen. Sie soll in 2 Etappen vor sich gehen. Die

Juden

T e l e g r a m m
(G-Schreiber)

B u d a p e s t , den 11. Juli 1944 15.15 Uhr
Ankunft, den 11. Juli 1944 19.30 Uhr

Nr. 1927 vom 11.7.44.

G e h e i m !

+) Inl II a (V.S.)

Im Anschluß an Fernschreiben Nr. 1838 +) vom 30. Juni.

I. Konzentrierung und Abtransport Juden in Zone V einschließlich Aktion Vorstädte Budapest am 9. Juli planmäßig mit 55.741 abgeschlossen. Gesamtziffer aus Zonen I bis V einschließlich Vorstadtaktion nunmehr 437.402.

II. Über Fortgang Aktion gegen Budapest ist gesondert nach Fuschl berichtet worden.

Veesenmayer

July 11, 1944 telegram from the German plenipotentiary delegate in Hungary, Edmund Veesenmayer, to the German foreign ministry. Veesenmayer reports that 437,402 Jews have been deported from Hungary through July 9, 1944.

Radiogram of March 24, 1942 from the SS Main Office for Economic and Administrative Matters (SS-WVHA), informing the commandant of Auschwitz Concentration Camp about the dispatch to the camp of trains carrying 10,000 Jewish women from Slovakia. Each train was to carry one thousand women, and the schedule had been agreed with the German railways.

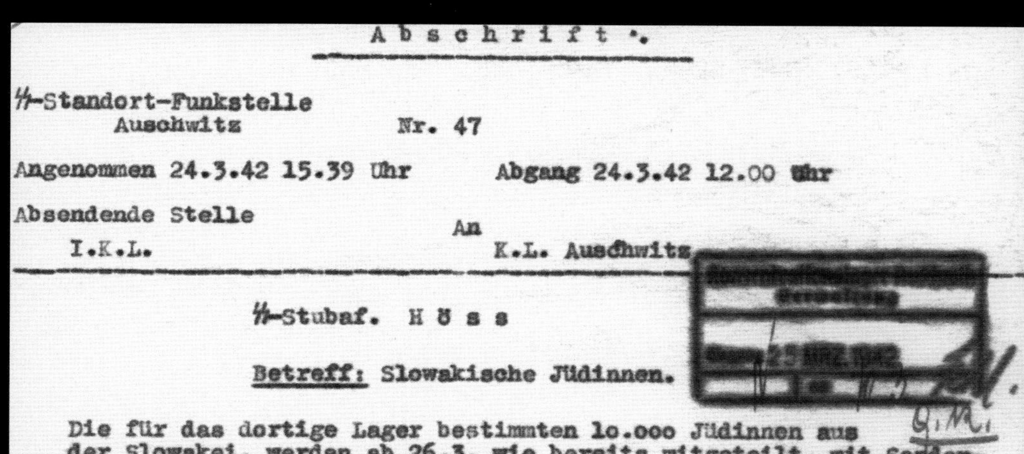

A b s c h r i f t .

ᛋᛋ-Standort-Funkstelle
Auschwitz Nr. 47

Angenommen 24.3.42 15.39 Uhr Abgang 24.3.42 12.00 Uhr

Absendende Stelle An
I.K.L. K.L. Auschwitz

ᛋᛋ-Stubaf. H ö s s

Betreff: Slowakische Jüdinnen.

Die für das dortige Lager bestimmten 10.000 Jüdinnen aus der Slowakei, werden ab 26.3. wie bereits mitgeteilt, mit Sonderzügen nach dort überstellt werden. Jeder Sonderzug führt 1000 Häftlinge mit. Alle Züge werden über den Grenzbahnhof Z w a r d o n , (Oberschlesien) geleitet, wo sie jeweils 6,09 Uhr früh eintreffen und während eines 2stündigen Aufenthaltes von Begleitkommandos der Schutzpolizei unter Aufsicht der Staatspolizei-Leitstelle Kattowitz, übernommen und an die Bestimmungsorte weitergeleitet werden. Die Führer der Begleitkommandos führen namentliche Transportlisten mit. Mit der Reichsbahn werden zunächst für die ersten 4 Transporte folgende Fahrpläne vereinbahrt. Da, da 66 am 26.3./ Da. da 68 am 28.3./ Da. da 71 am 2.4./ Da.da 73 am 3.4.an diesen Ta-

Pass dispatching a truck to Dessau to pick up material for special treatment ("*Material für Sonderbehandlung*"), as the extermination of human beings in the gas chambers was described in the camp records.

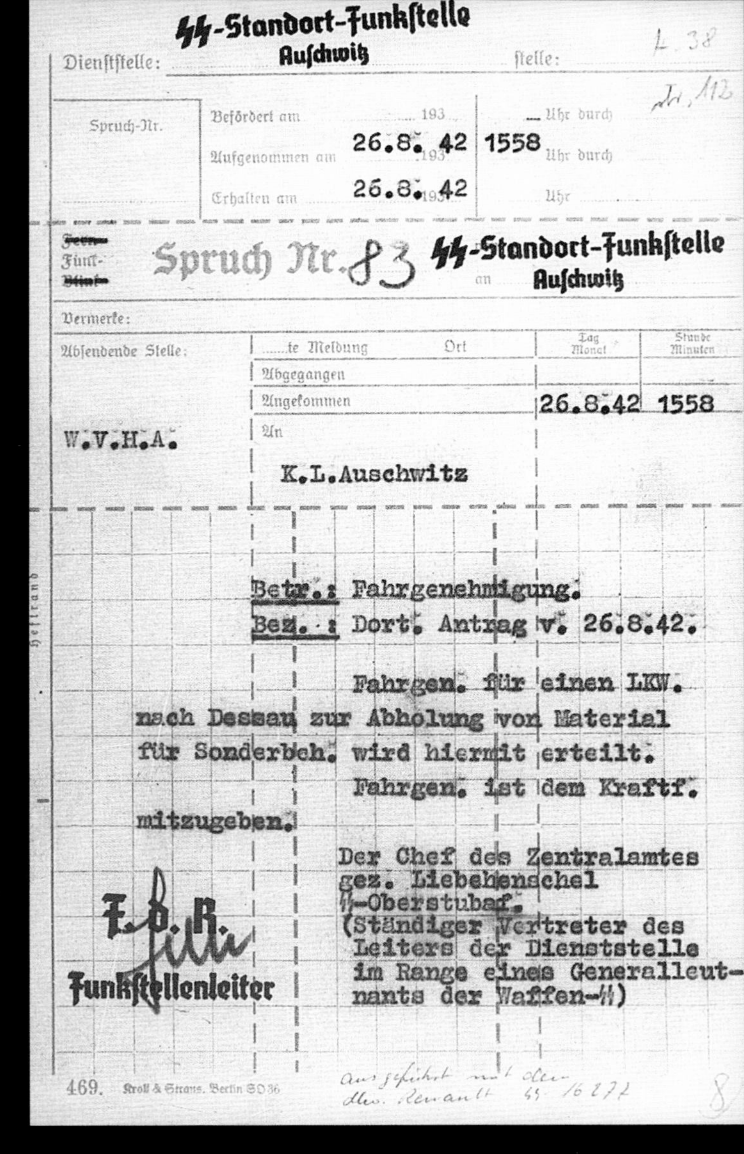

SS-Standort-Funkstelle Auschwitz

Dienststelle: ... stelle:

Spruch-Nr.	Befördert am ... 193	Uhr durch
	Aufgenommen am 26.8.42	1558 Uhr durch
	Erhalten am 26.8.42	Uhr

Spruch Nr. 83 — SS-Standort-Funkstelle an Auschwitz

Vermerke:

Absendende Stelle:	...te Meldung Ort	Tag Monat	Stunde Minuten
	Abgegangen		
	Angekommen	26.8.42	1558
W.V.H.A.	An K.L.Auschwitz		

Betr.: Fahrgenehmigung.
Bez.: Dort. Antrag v. 26.8.42.

Fahrgen. für einen LKW. nach Dessau zur Abholung von Material für Sonderbeh. wird hiermit erteilt. Fahrgen. ist dem Kraftf. mitzugeben.

Der Chef des Zentralamtes
gez. Liebehenschel
SS-Oberstubaf.
(Ständiger Vertreter des Leiters der Dienststelle im Range eines Generalleutnants der Waffen-SS)

F.d.R.
Funkstellenleiter

469. Kroll & Strauss, Berlin SO 36

At left:
Auschwitz I.
The building containing the first crematorium, which the SS put into operation in the summer of 1940.

Zyklon-B, in the form of granules of diatomaceous earth impregnated with hydrogen cyanide, was supplied in canisters of various sizes. It was produced by the Degesch company and distributed by Tesch und Stabenow of Dessau.

Auschwitz I.
The first gas chamber, set up in the morgue of Crematorium I at the end of 1941 or the beginning of 1942.

Auschwitz I.
The interior of the crematorium.

Auschwitz I. The interior of the crematorium. Reconstructed ovens for burning corpses; one of the places for commemorating and paying tribute to the victims of the camp. Photograph taken on All Soul's Day in November.

Auschwitz II – Birkenau.
Arrival of a transport of Jews from Hungary at the special railroad spur and unloading "ramp"
(SS photograph, 1944).

Men and women had to line up separately. These orders struck everyone like lightning. Now, in the final stage, when the end of the road had been reached, they ordered the dividing, the sundering, of the inseparable. They ordered the sundering of the inseparable, of what had been joined together and grown into a single indivisible whole. No one took a step, for no one could believe in something that was unbelievable. It could not be that the unreal had become real, a fact. Yet the hail of blows that fell upon the first rank of the people standing there made such an impact that families began to draw apart even in the rows at the back. . . . They supposed that the formal procedure of precisely determining the number of new arrivals was beginning, the two sexes separately. They sensed that the most important moment was now approaching, when it would be necessary to comfort each other and give consolation.

From the manuscript of the Jewish prisoner Załmen Gradowski, discovered after the war at the site of the camp.

A transport of Jews from Hungary (SS photo, 1944).

SS men form newly arrived Jews into two columns on the ramp—men in one column, women and children in the other (SS photo, 1944).

Auschwitz II – Birkenau. The railroad spur and the ramp where the SS received newly arrived transports of Jews. The crematoria chimneys can no longer be seen on the horizon, since these buildings were destroyed by the retreating SS as part of the effort to remove evidence of their crimes.

From the memoirs of Unterscharführer Pery Broad, an SS man in the camp Gestapo.

First of all, the men and women are separated. Dreadful scenes of farewell occur. Married couples are separated and mothers wave to their sons for the last time.
The columns stand on the ramp, in rows of five, several meters apart. When someone succumbs to the pain of farewell and runs one last time to the other column in order to reach out a hand to the beloved and whisper a few comforting words, the SS man instantly rains down blows and shoves that person back in place. Now the SS physician begins the division into those who, in his opinion, are capable of labor, and those who are not. Mothers with little children are regarded on principle as incapable of labor, as are all those who give an impression of being frail or sick. Portable wooden stairs are placed at the backs of trucks and those selected by the SS physician as unfit for labor must climb in.
The SS men from the reception department count them as they go up the steps one by one. In the same way, they next count all those fit for labor, who must set out on the march to the men's or women's camp. All the baggage must be left on the ramp. The prisoners are told that it will later be delivered by truck. This is true so far as it goes, except that none of the prisoners will see their belongings again, and everything will end up in the safes, warehouses, and SS kitchens. Smaller bags containing essential items and whatever they are wearing will be taken from them later, when they are received into the camp.

Auschwitz II – Birkenau. Selection on the ramp. As they saw fit, on the basis of a cursory evaluation, SS physicians and nurses chose those from among the newly arrived Jews who were fit for labor...

...and sent them to the camp. The others, most often 70 to 75%, were designated for immediate death in the gas chambers (SS photo, 1944).

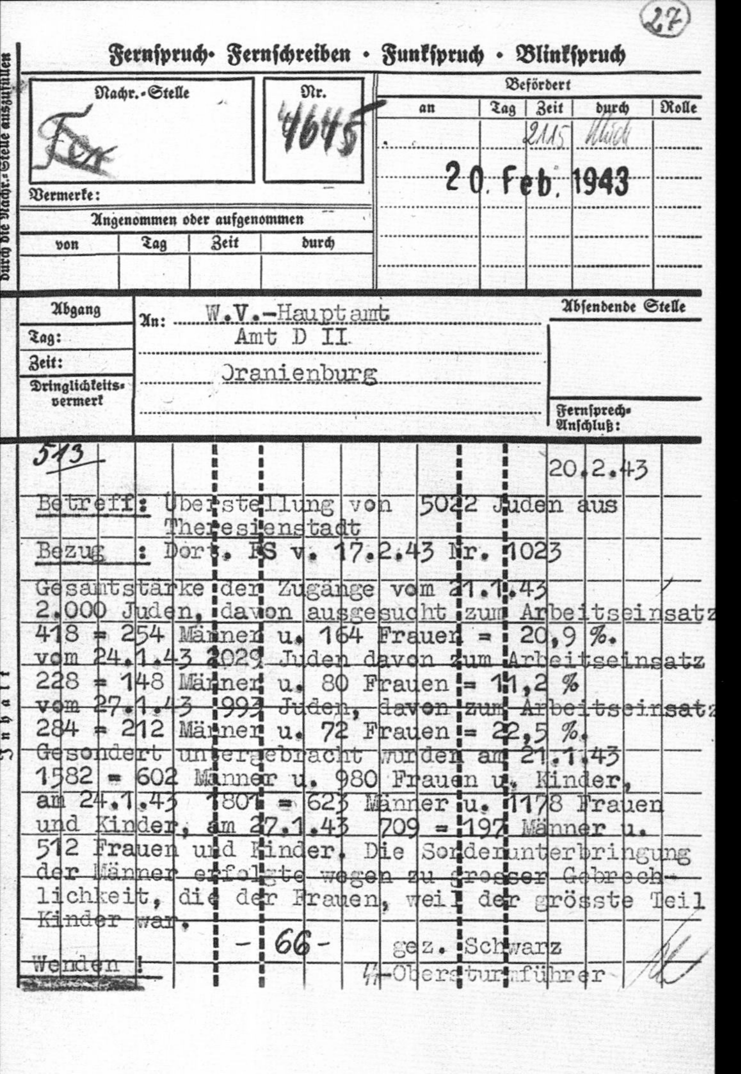

(27)

Fernspruch · Fernschreiben · Funkspruch · Blinkspruch

Durch die Nachr.-Stelle auszufüllen

Nachr.-Stelle: Fer — Nr.: 4645

Befördert: an | Tag | Zeit 2115 | durch | Rolle

20 Feb. 1943

Vermerke:

Angenommen oder aufgenommen: von | Tag | Zeit | durch

Abgang — Tag: — Zeit: — Dringlichkeitsvermerk

An: W.V.-Hauptamt
Amt D II
Oranienburg

Absendende Stelle

Fernsprech-Anschluß:

Inhalt

513 20.2.43

Betreff: Überstellung von 5022 Juden aus Theresienstadt

Bezug : Dort. FS v. 17.2.43 Nr. 1023

Gesamtstärke der Zugänge vom 21.1.43
2.000 Juden, davon ausgesucht zum Arbeitseinsatz
418 = 254 Männer u. 164 Frauen = 20,9 %.
vom 24.1.43 2029 Juden davon zum Arbeitseinsatz
228 = 148 Männer u. 80 Frauen = 11,2 %
vom 27.1.43 993 Juden, davon zum Arbeitseinsatz
284 = 212 Männer u. 72 Frauen = 22,5 %.
Gesondert untergebracht wurden am 21.1.43
1582 = 602 Männer u. 980 Frauen u. Kinder,
am 24.1.43 1801 = 623 Männer u. 1178 Frauen
und Kinder, am 27.1.43 709 = 197 Männer u.
512 Frauen und Kinder. Die Sonderunterbringung
der Männer erfolgte wegen zu grosser Gebrechlichkeit, die der Frauen, weil der grösste Teil
Kinder war.

- 66 -

gez. Schwarz
SS-Obersturmführer

Wenden !

A precise report on the delivery of Jews from Theresienstadt to Auschwitz:
"Regarding: Dispatch of 5,022 Jews from Theresienstadt.
In reference to: Dort. telegram no. 1023 of Feb. 17, 1943
From among the Jews arriving Jan. 21, 1943 numbering 2,000:
selected for work:
418 = 254 men and 164 women = 20.9%
Jan. 24, 1943 – 2,029 Jews, of which for work 228 = 148 men and 80 women = 11.2%
Jan. 27, 1943 – 993 Jews, of which for work 284 = 212 men and 72 women = 22.5%.
Jan. 21, 1943 separate disposition 1,582 = 602 men and 980 women and children, Jan. 24, 1943 – 1,801 = 623 men and 1,178 women and children, Jan. 27, 1943 – 709 = 197 men and 512 women and children. Separate disposition of the men was caused by their excessive frailty, and of the women, because the majority of them were children."

Auschwitz II – Birkenau. Selection of newly arrived Jews by SS medical personnel (SS photo, 1944).

Auschwitz II – Birkenau. Selection (SS photo,1944).

Auschwitz II – Birkenau.

Auschwitz II – Birkenau.
The road that led
women and children to death
in the gas chambers.

Headline from the *Ostschweizerisches Tagblatt* [The East-Swiss Daily]:
"Trains Full of Jewish Children – Bound Where?"

Ostschweizerisches Tagblatt
und
Rorschacher Tagblatt

(des Ostschweizerischen Wochenblattes 102. Jahrgang)

62 EISENBAHNEN VOLL JÜDISCHE KINDER... WOHIN?

London, 8. Juli. (Reuter.) Das polnische Innenministerium hat vom Delegierten der polnischen Regierung in Polen Einzelheiten über das Schicksal der aus Ungarn deportierten 400.000 Juden erfahren. Der grösste Teil der Deportierten wurde nach dem Vernichtungslager von Auschwitz in Oberschlesien übergeführt. Am 15. Mai wurden von den Deutschen in Ungarn 62 Eisenbahnwagen mit jüdischen Kinder im Alter von 2 bis 8 Jahren abtransportiert und seither verliessen täglich Eisenbahnzüge mit Erwachsenen den Bahnhof von Plaszow bei Krakau.

Nach den beim polnischen Hilfskomitee für die Juden in Polen vorliegenden Informationen sind seit dem Jahre 1939 2 Millionen polnische Juden in drei Konzentrationslagern Polens ums Leben gekommen.

Diese Reutermeldung wird auch von der Exchange-Agentur verbreitet mit folgenden Zusätzen:

„Es konnte festgestellt werden, dass die meisten der durchfahrenden Erwachsenen nach Oswiecim geschafft und in den Gaskammern des Lagers hingerichtet wurden." Die polnische Regierung warnt, Briefen, aus denen hervorgeht, dass der Schreiber anscheinend guten Mutes ist, und die aus Oswiecim datiert sind, Glauben zu schenken. Es sei festgestellt worden, dass diese Briefe erzwungen wurden. Das polnische Innenministerium stellte ferner die tägliche Vergasungskapazität in den Kammern von Oswiecim mit 6000 fest. Das Innenministerium erklärt schliesslich, dass in der zweiten Hälfte des Jahres 1942 zwei weitere Todeslager von den Deutschen in Polen errichtet wurden, das Lager Tremblinka und das Lager Rawaruska. Ob auch dort Gaskammern eingerichtet wurden, sei unbekannt.

Die Massenmorde an den Juden wurden übrigens bis heute von deutscher Seite gar nicht bestritten; sie liegen ganz in der Linie der von Hitler ausgegebenen Parole, das Judentum müsse „ausgerottet" werden.

Los Angeles Times

EQUAL RIGHTS

LIBERTY UNDER THE LAW — TRUE INDUSTRIAL FREEDOM

WEDNESDAY MORNING, MARCH 22, 1944

Poles Report Mass Murder

LONDON, March 21. (AP)—The Polish Ministry of Information said today that more than 500,000 persons, mostly Jews, had been put to death at a concentration camp at Osweicim, southwest of Krakow.

In a lengthy report on Nazi atrocities the ministry declared three crematoriums had been erected inside the camp to dispose of 10,000 bodies a day. Gas chambers were said to have been attached to the crematoriums.

The report asserted that men, women and children arrive by truckloads and are removed to the gas chambers where 10 to 15 minutes are required for execution, but since the supply of poison gas is limited some persons are not dead when they are thrown into the crematorium.

The Polish resistance movement and government-in-exile informed the Allies about the Nazi crimes in Auschwitz. Articles on the subject appeared in the western press, in Switzerland, the USA, and other countries, in 1944.

Auschwitz II – Birkenau. The middle part of the ramp where newly arrived Jews were selected.

Auschwitz II – Birkenau. The gate leading to the grounds of gas chamber and crematorium II. The ruins of the building, demolished by the SS, are visible in the background.

"They were packed in [as tightly as possible]. It was hard to even imagine that so many people could fit into such a small [room]. Everyone who tried to get out was shot [for resisting] or torn apart by the dogs. Asphyxiation from lack of air would have come within a few hours. Then all the doors were closed tight and the gas was thrown in through a small window in the ceiling. The people locked inside could do nothing. So they only cried out in bitter, mournful voices. Others complained in voices full of despair, and still others sobbed spasmodically and sent up a dreadful, piercing crying. Some recited the "widduj" or cried out "Shema Israel." All of them tore out their hair for having been so naìve as to have allowed themselves to be led there, to those closed doors. Only one idea came to them, to utter in voices that rose to the heavens their last cry of protest against the greatest of historical injustices, which was inflicted on completely innocent people only in order to destroy whole generations all at once in such a terrible manner. . . . Because of the great overcrowding, the dying people fell one upon the other, until a heap rose up of five to six layers one atop the other to the height of a meter. Mothers froze in a sitting position on the ground holding their children in their arms, and husbands and wives died in an embrace. Some of the people formed a shapeless mass...

From the notes of the Jewish prisoner Lejb (Langfus), written illegally in the camp and buried next to Crematorium III. After liberation, the manuscript was found next to the ruins of the crematorium and placed in the Museum Archives.

Women and children being led towards gas and V after selection (SS photo, 1944).

Auschwitz II – Birkenau. Women and children being led to their death in the gas chambers after selection. (SS photo, 1944.)

From the notebook of the Jewish prisoner Leib (Langfus).

... Others stood leaning over, with the lower parts of their bodies in a standing position and the upper part, from the abdomen up, prone. Some of the people were completely blue under the influence of the gas, while others looked absolutely fresh, as if they were asleep. Not all of them fit in the bunker; some of them were held in a wooden barracks until eleven o'clock the next day. They heard the despairing cries of the people being gassed in the small hours, and realized at once what lay in store for them. They looked upon it all and experienced the most horrible anguish in the world during that accursed night and half of the next day. No one who has not experienced something of the sort can have the faintest idea about this. As I later learned, my wife and son were also in that group. The Sonder [kommando], which was then divided into four groups and composed exclusively of Jews, appeared early in the morning. Having put on gas masks, the first group entered the bunker and threw out the bodies of those who had been gassed. Another group dragged the bodies to the tracks where wagons without side rails waited. The next group loaded the bodies onto the little wagons, called "lorries," and pushed them to a certain point where a great, wide, deep pit had been dug, lined [on all sides] with blocks, beams, and whole trees. Gasoline [was poured on] and a hellish flame belched forth. . . . The fourth group stood there throwing the people into the fire. They burned [until] they had been completely reduced [to ashes]. Of the whole transport, there remained a small [pile] of charred bones, which were pushed off to the side. Not even that small remnant of bones was left in peace. They were thrown out of the pit. . . . They were to become like ashes dumped [on the] ground. On the surface of the ground [trees] were planted in this place, so that no sign of human life should remain.

Auschwitz II – Birkenau. The foundations of one of the first gas chambers, known in the camp as bunker no. 2 or "the little white house."

"The victims generally behaved calmly, even though in 1943 most already knew their fates. There were instances of revolt or mass escape attempts while getting off the wagons, but they were always bloodily crushed. The unloading platform (specially built for this) was ringed with spotlights and machine gun nests. There was only a single case when a self-defense action had some result. It was in September or October 1943. A transport of women arrived at the crematorium at night. The convoying SS-men fell among them, ordering them to undress and herding them to the chambers. This is the best tactic for theft, taking rings from fingers, removing watches, etc. The ones doing this had to torment the one they picked out, in order to have an explanation for their presence there, to keep up the appearance that they were only performing their official function. In the ensuring confusion one of the women jerked away the revolver of *Unterscharführer* Schilinger [Schillinger], seriously wounding him with three bullets (he died the next day), which was a signal for the rest to throw themselves on the SS-men. One of them got his nose bit off and another got his scalp split by the women. None of them were saved, though."

From the report written by the Polish political prisoner Jerzy Tabeau after his escape from the camp in 1943.

At right: Auschwitz II – Birkenau. The beams and ceiling of the hall containing the furnaces.

Auschwitz II – Birkenau. Crematorium and gas chamber II went into operation on March 31, 1943 (SS photo, 1943).

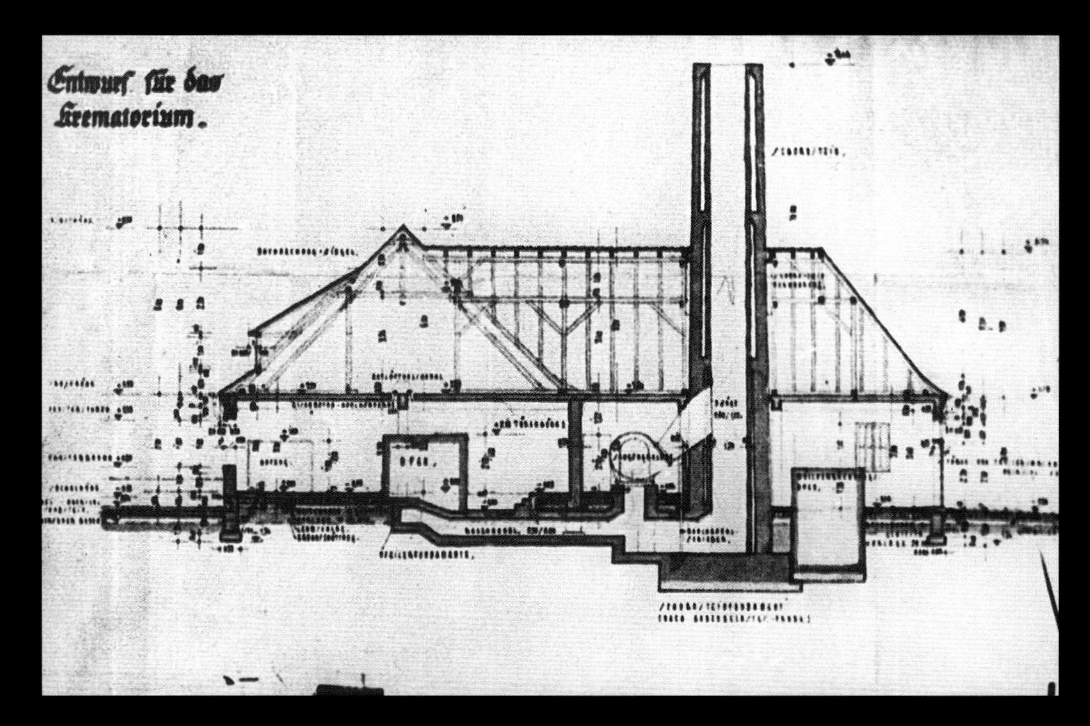

Photocopy of German blueprints for crematoria II and III, dated January 27, 1942.

From the memoirs of the Auschwitz camp commandant, SS-Obersturmbannführer Rudolf Höß.

"The extermination process in Auschwitz took place as follows:
Jews selected for gassing were taken as quietly as possible to the crematoria, the men being separated from the women. In the undressing room prisoners of the special detachment, detailed for this purpose, would tell them in their own language that they were going to be bathed and deloused, that they must leave their clothes neatly together and above all remember where they had put them, so that they would be able to find them again quickly after delousing. The prisoners of the special detachment had the greatest interest in seeing that the operation proceeded smoothly and quickly. After undressing, the Jews went into the gas chambers, which were furnished with showers and water pipes and gave a realistic impression of a bath-house.
The women went first with their children, followed by the men who were always fewer in number. This part of the operation nearly always went smoothly, to the prisoners of the special detachment would calm those who betrayed any anxiety or who perhaps had some inkling of their fate. As an additional precaution these prisoners of the special detachment and an SS-man always remained in the chamber until the last moment.
The door would now be quickly screwed up and the gas immediately discharged by the waiting disinfectors through vents in the ceiling of the gas chambers, down a shaft that led to the floor. This ensured the rapid distribution of the gas. It could be observed through the peep-in in the door that those who were standing nearest to the induction vents were killed at once. It can be said that about one third died straight away. The remainders staggered about and began to scream and struggle for air. The screaming, however, soon changed to the death rattle and in a few minutes all lay still. After twenty minutes at the latest no movement could be discerned. The time required on whether it was damp or dry, cold or warm. It also depended on the quality of the gas, which was never exactly the same, and on the composition of the transports which might contain a high proportion of healthy Jews, or old and sick, or children. The victims became unconscious after a few minutes, according to their distance from the intake shaft. Those who screamed and those who were old or sick or weak, or the small children, died quicker than those who were healthy or young.
The door was opened half an hour after the induction of the gas, and the ventilation switched on. Work was immediately begun on removing the corpses. There was no noticeable change in the bodies and no sign of convulsions or discoloration. Only after the bodies had been left lying for some time, that is to say after several hours, did the usual death stains appear in the places where they had lain. Soling through opening to the bowels was also rare. There were no signs of wounding of any kind. The faces showed no distortion.
The special detachment now set about removing the gold teeth and cutting the hair from the women. After this, the bodies were taken up by lift and laid in front of the ovens, which had meanwhile been stoked up.."

Auschwitz II – Birkenau. The collapsed roof beams of the underground gas chamber, which was blown up by the SS before the liberation of the camp.

Auschwitz II – Birkenau. The railroad spur and unloading ramp inside the camp, built in 1944. Trains carrying deportees to the camp came here through the main SS guardhouse, known as the Gate of Death.

Auschwitz II – Birkenau. Roll call of newly arrived Jewish women selected on the ramp as fit for labor.

Auschwitz II – Birkenau. The ruins of crematorium II. The floor of the furnace room and traces of the tracks used to carry bodies to the furnaces are visible.

"600 boys were led there in the middle of one bright day, 600 Jewish boys aged 12 to 18, dressed in very thin, long striped camp uniforms, with ragged boots or wooden clogs on their feet. The boys looked so beautiful and were so well built that not even those rags could make them look bad. This was in the second half of October [1944]. 25 SS men, heavily loaded down [with hand grenades] led them in. When they reached the square, the Kommandoführer ordered them to dis[robe]. . . . The boys saw the smoke belching from the chimney and realized instantly that they were being led to their death. They began running around the square in wild horror, tearing out their hair, [not know]ing how to save themselves. Many of them broke down in grievous weeping, a terrible lament [went up]. The Kommandoführer and his helper beat the defenseless boys mercilessly to make them disrobe. His club broke from that beating. So he fetched another one and kept beating them over their heads until his violence won out. The boys disrobed with an instinctive dread of death, and huddled together naked and barefoot in order to protect themselves from the blows, and they did not move. Many of the boys made a wild dash towards [the Jews] from the Sonderkommando and threw their arms around their necks pleading for salvation. Others ran naked around that large square [to escape] death. The Kommandoführer called on the Unterscharführer to help with his rubber club. . . .
The clear young voices of the boys grew louder by the minute [until they changed into] bitter crying. That terrible lament carried far."

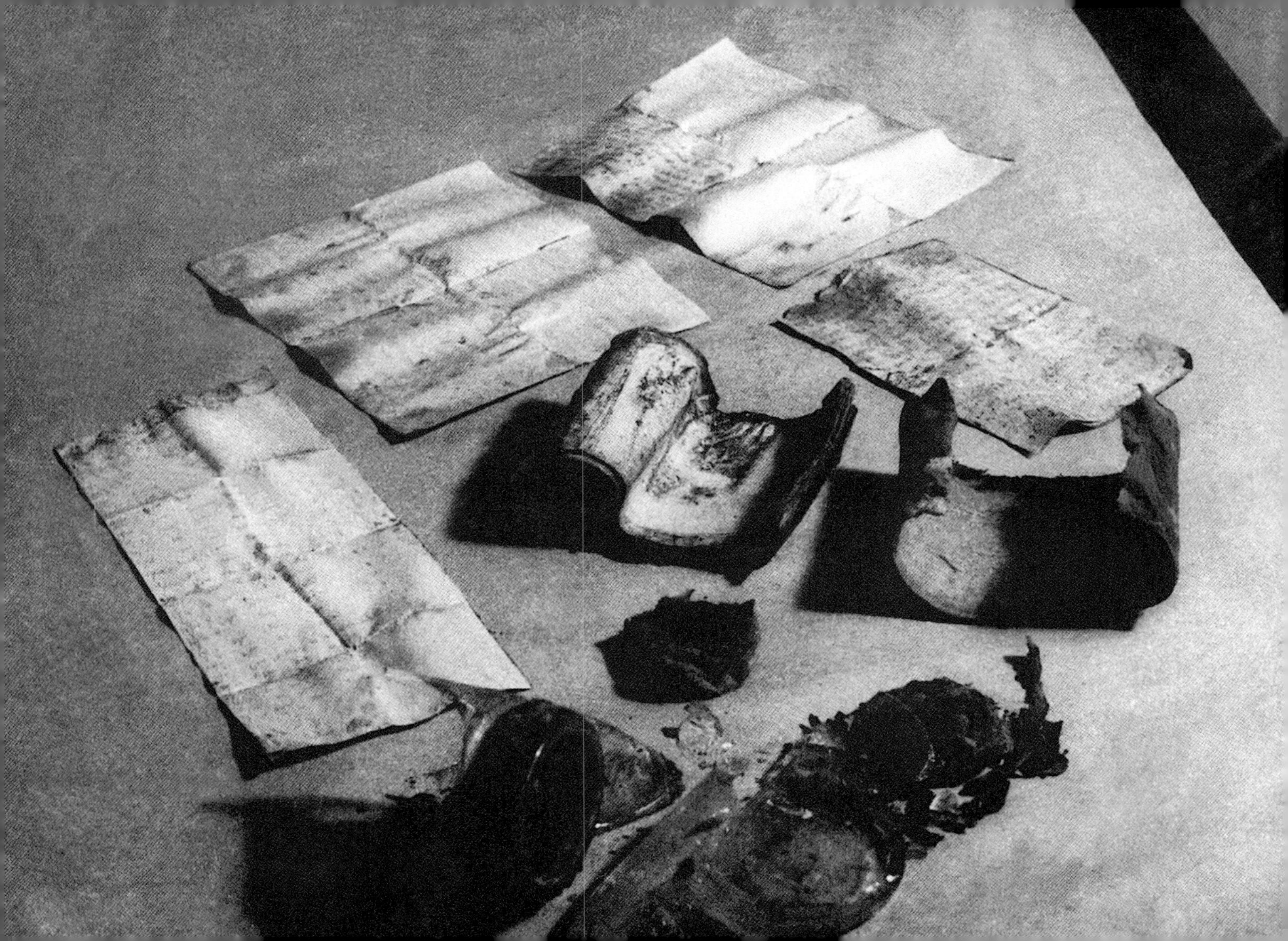

Auschwitz II – Birkenau. The woods surrounding Crematorium V (ruins visible behind the trees). Mothers with small children waited among these trees for places in the gas chambers.

At right: Auschwitz II – Birkenau. The steps leading down to the underground undressing room in Crematorium III.

Auschwitz II – Birkenau. Waiting for death in the gas chambers in Crematoria IV and V. (SS photo, 1944.)

Auschwitz II – Birkenau. (SS photo, 1944.)

Auschwitz II – Birkenau. The remains of the gas chambers and crematorium IV. This building was destroyed during the mutiny by Jewish prisoners from the special labor detail (*Sonderkommando*). This labor detail was employed to remove the bodies of murdered people from the gas chambers and burn them in furnaces or in the open air. On October 7, 1944, the Jews in the *Sonderkommando* organized a desperate mutiny, the only armed rebellion in the camp. Three SS men died in the fighting and Crematorium IV was completely destroyed. The majority of the prisoners in the labor detail perished during the fighting or under interrogation.

From the manuscript of the Jewish prisoner Załmen Levental. All the accounts known so far of the mutiny of October 7, 1944 differ in details, since none of the authors of the accounts was a direct participant.

"We reinforced our position for the last time and clearly and precisely informed the people who were in contact with us how they were to behave in various circumstances. When they arrived at 1:25 p.m. to take those three hundred people away, they showed enormous courage and refused to move. They sent up an enormous shout, and fell upon the guards with sledge hammers and hatchets, wounding some of them, while the others fought any way they could, simply throwing stones at them. It was easy to imagine what would happen next. Not more than a few moments passed before an entire unit of SS men, armed with automatic rifles and hand grenades, arrived. There were so many of them that they had no less than two automatic rifles for every prisoner. Such was the army they mobilized against us. Seeing that they were lost, our people wanted in the last moment to burn down Crematorium IV and die fighting, to fall on the spot beneath the hail of bullets. And in that way, the whole crematorium went up in smoke."

Auschwitz II – Birkenau. Part of the camp.

Auschwitz II – Birkenau. Crematorium and gas chamber IV went into operation on March 22, 1943. In this building, the gas chambers and the large eightfold furnace for burning the corpses were located on a single floor (SS photo, 1943).

Auschwitz II – Birkenau.
View of the camp from the north.

Auschwitz II – Birkenau. The ruins of crematorium V – the part where the large eightfold furnace and two chimneys were located.

Auschwitz II – Birkenau. The ruins of Crematorium V, with the remains of one of the gas chambers in the foreground.

Photograph taken covertly by a *Sonderkommando* prisoner, probably the Greek Jew Alex, in 1944. Women being led to the gas chamber in Crematorium V.

Secret message written on September 4, 1944 by the Polish political prisoners Józef Cyrankiewicz and Stanisław Kłodziński and sent to the Polish resistance movement in Cracow.

Auschwitz II – Birkenau. Corpses being burned in the open air (Photograph taken covertly by a *Sonderkommando* prisoner, probably the Greek Jew Alex, 1944).

Auschwitz I. Part of the permanent exhibition in Block no. 4 – a display case containing the hair of victims and haircloth woven from human hair.

German firms paid 0.50 marks per kilogram of hair.

Approximately 7,000 kilograms of hair were found in warehouses after the liberation of the camp in January 1945. The hair was packed in paper sacks, ready to be shipped for processing in German factories (Photo from the inspection of the warehouses full of hair by the Soviet State Commission for the Investigation of the Crimes of the German-Fascist Aggressors).

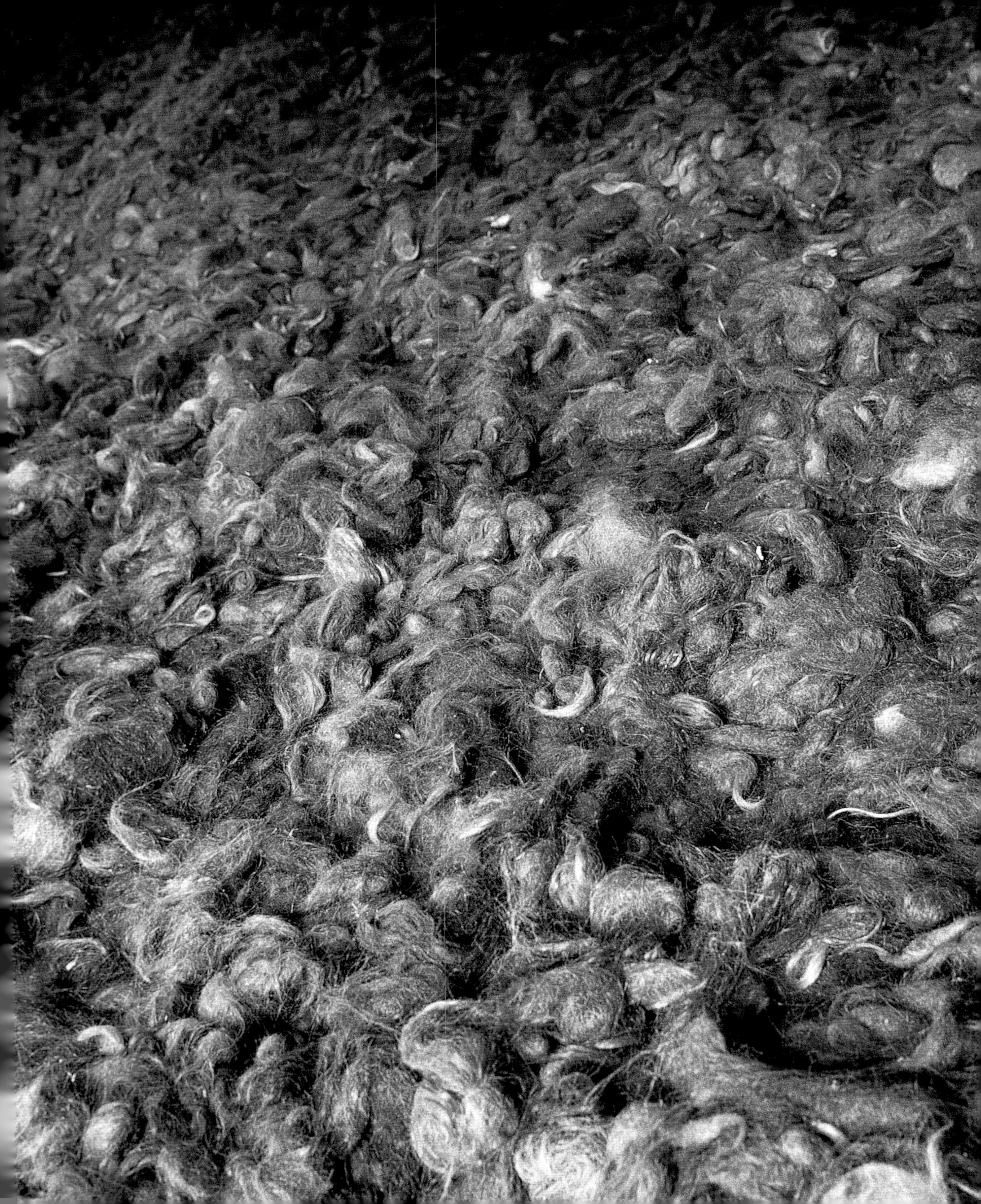

Auschwitz II – Birkenau. Newly arrived
Jews on the ramp in Birkenau
(SS photo, 1944).

Auschwitz II – Birkenau. Fringed garments found after the liberation of the camp, now in the permanent exhibition in Block no. 5, devoted to the mass extermination of the Jews.

The so-called "Sauna," or main camp bathhouse. Procedures connected with the reception of prisoners in the camp were carried out here, including the shaving of their heads, the tattooing of prisoner numbers, and the distribution of striped camp uniforms. Garments confiscated from the people who were murdered were also cleaned and disinfected in this building before being shipped into the depths of the Third Reich.

Auschwitz II – Birkenau. The interior of the camp "Sauna" – equipment for cleaning and disinfecting clothing with the use of steam or hot air.

From the memoirs of the Auschwitz camp commandant, SS-Obersturmbannführer Rudolf Höß.

"The jewellery was usually of great value, particularly if its Jewish owners came from the west: precious stones worth thousands of pounds, priceless gold and platinum watches set with diamonds, rings, earrings and necklaces of great rarity. Currency from all countries amounted to many thousands of pounds. Often tens of thousands of pounds in value, mostly in thousand-dollar notes, were found on single individuals. Every possible hiding place in their clothes and luggage and on their bodies was made use of. When the sorting process that followed each major operation had been completed, the valuables and money ware packed into trunks and taken by lorry to the Economic and Administrative Head Office in Berlin and thence to the Reichsbank, where a special department dealt exclusively with items taken during action against the Jews. Eichmann told me on one occasion that the jewellery and currency were sold in Switzerland, and that the entire Swiss jewellery market was dominated by these sales.
Ordinary watches were likewise sent in their thousands to Sachsenhausen. A large watchmaker's shop had been set up there, which employed hundreds of prisoners and was directly administered by the Department DII (Maurer). The watches were sorted out and repaired in the workshop, the majority being later dispatched for service use by front-line SS and army troops.
Gold from the teeth was melted into bars by the dentists in the SS hospital and forwarded monthly to the Sanitary Head Office.
Precious stones of great value were also to be found hidden in teeth that had been stopped.
Hair cut from the women was sent to a firm in Bavaria to be used in the war effort.".

"When the Jewish transports unloaded on arrival, their luggage was left on the platform until all the Jews had been taken to the extermination buildings or into the camp" (R. Höß).

Auschwitz II – Birkenau. The plundered possessions of the victims of mass extermination were stored and sorted in a special separate part of the camp that the prisoners called "Kanada" (SS photo, 1944).

Abschrift Geheim

Aufstellung

über die von den Lagern Lublin und Auschwitz auf Anordnung des W...
schafts-Verwaltungshauptamt abgelieferten Mengen an Textil-Altma...

1. Reichswirtschaftsministerium

Männer-Altbekleidung ohne Wäsche	97 000 Garnituren	
Frauen-Altbekleidung ohne Wäsche	76 000 Garnituren	
Frauen-Seidenwäsche	89 000 Garnituren	
	insgesamt:	34 Wag...

Lumpen	400 Waggons	2 700 000 kg
Bettfedern	130 Waggons	270 000 kg
Frauenhaare	1 Waggon	3 000 kg
Altmaterial	5 Waggons	19 000 kg
	insgesamt:	2 992 000 kg

insgesamt: 536 Wag...

570 Wag...

2. Volksdeutsche Mittelstelle

Männerbekleidung:		Kinderbekleidung:	
Mäntel	99 000 Stck.	Mäntel	15 000 Stck.
Röcke	57 000 "	Knabenröcke	11 000 "
Westen	27 000 "	Knabenhosen	3 000 "
Hosen	62 000 "	Hemden	3 000 "
Unterhosen	38 000 "	Schals	4 000 "
Hemden	132 000 "	Pullover	1 000 "
Pullover	9 000 "	Unterhosen	1 000 "
Schals	2 000 "	Mädchenkleider	9 000 "
Pyjamas	6 000 "	Mädchenhemden	5 000 "
Kragen	10 000 "	Schürzen	2 000 "
Handschuhe	2 000 Paar	Schlüpfer	5 000 "
Strümpfe	10 000 "	Strümpfe	10 000 Paar
Schuhe	31 000 "	Schuhe	22 000 "

Frauenbekleidung:		Wäsche usw.:	
Mäntel	155 000 Stck.	Bettbezüge	37 000 Stck.
Kleider	119 000 "	Bettlaken	46 000 "
Jacken	26 000 "	Kopfkissen-bezüge	75 000 "
Röcke	30 000 "	Geschirrtücher	27 000 "
Hemden	125 000 "	Taschentücher	135 000 "
Blusen	30 000 "	Handtücher	100 000 "
Pullover	60 000 "	Tischdecken	11 000 "
Unterhosen	49 000 "	Servietten	8 000 "
Schlüpfer	60 000 "	Wolltücher	6 000 "
Pyjamas	27 000 "	Krawatten	25 000 "
Schürzen	36 000 "	Gummischuhe und Stiefel	24 000 Paar
Büstenhalter	25 000 "	Mützen	9 000 Stck.
Unterkleider	22 000 "		
Kopftücher	85 000 "		
Schuhe	111 000 Paar	insgesamt:	211 Wag...

Part of a secret report by the head of the Main SS Economic-Administrative Office, Oswald Pohl, dated February 2, 1943, on the dispatch from the Auschwitz and Majdanek camps of 825 train cars full of clothing and boots plundered from the victims of mass extermination, and one car full of women's hair.

Auschwitz II – Birkenau. Empty train cars and the Jewish deportees' possessions remain at the ramp (SS photo, 1944).

Auschwitz II – Birkenau. Sorting the victims' belongings in the "Kanada" warehouses (SS photo, 1944).

Auschwitz II – Birkenau.
Personal effects confiscated from the Jews on display at the exhibition in the camp "Sauna" building.

Auschwitz II – Birkenau.
Part of the exhibition in the camp "Sauna" building.

Auschwitz I. Suitcases found after liberation and displayed in the permanent exhibition in Block no. 5, devoted to the mass extermination of the Jews.

Auschwitz II – Birkenau.
Part of the exhibition in the camp "Sauna" building.

Auschwitz I.
Children's' clothing found after the liberation of the camp, displayed in the permanent exhibition in Block no. 5, devoted to the mass extermination of the Jews.

Auschwitz I.
Victims' clothing discovered at the moment the camp was liberated. (Chronicle of the liberation of the camp, 1945.)

The liberation of the camp: Soviet soldiers examining children's clothing.

Auschwitz II – Birkenau.
The burning "Kanada" warehouses, set ablaze by the SS men before they left the camp (Photo by Henryk Makarewicz, 1945).

Metal remains found at the site of the burned "Kanada" warehouses.

Auschwitz II – Birkenau.
Transport of Jews from
Hungary
(SS photo, 1944).

At right:
Auschwitz II –
Birkenau.
Part of the camp,
with the remains
of the wooden
barracks.

Auschwitz II – Birkenau. Over three hundred one-story prisoner barracks, mostly of wood, stood here when the camp was in existence (SS photo, 1944).

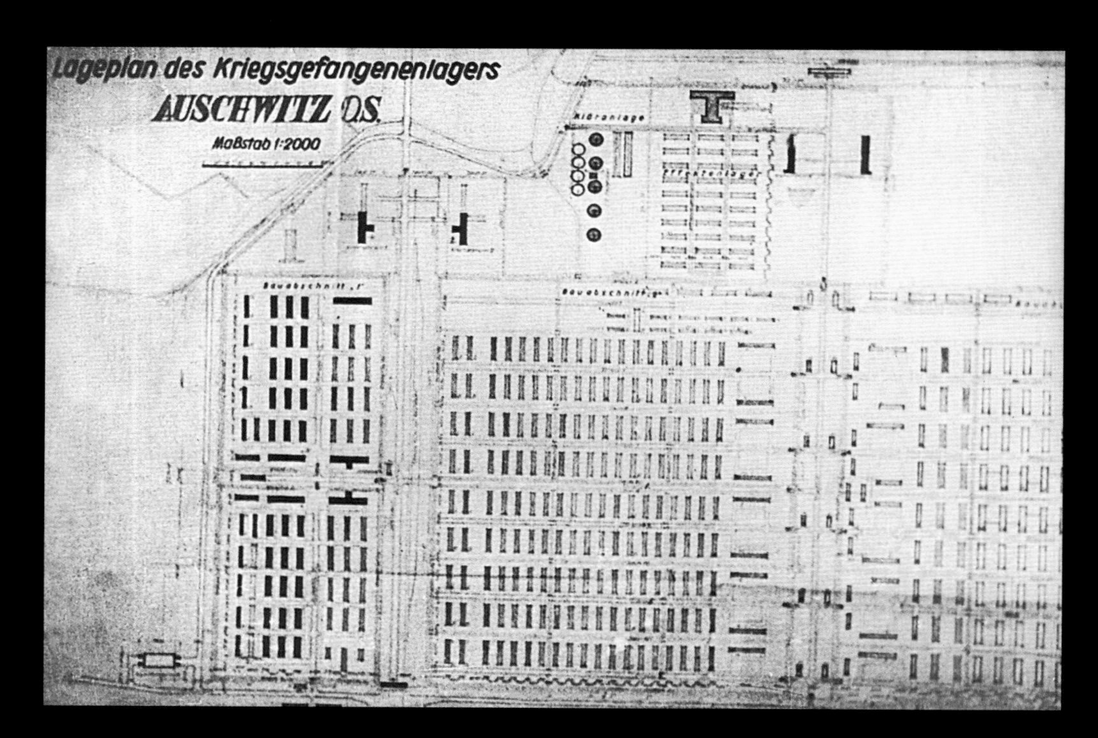

A German map of
the camp dated
March 20, 1943.

Auschwitz II – Birkenau. The outlines
of foundations and the hearths are
what remain from the majority
of the wooden barracks.

Auschwitz II – Birkenau. One of the places where the corpses of the people who had been murdered were burned in the open air. Their ashes are still here. The text on the stones reads: "In memory of men, women, and children, the victims of Nazi genocide. Their ashes are here. May they rest in peace."

"They were put in barracks meant to be horse stables. The blocks were not divided by any partitions, without windows, only small frosted panes high up near the ceiling. Between the roof and the walls, around the whole block, there were holes, very good as stable ventilators but not so suitable for people. Through these openings the rain and snow fell, the wind howled. The women sleeping near them often woke up at night soaked through or covered with a layer of snow. Since I later lived in a similar barrack, I have an idea of how it was in practice. For example, it is raining: the water spills not only through the openings on the side but also through the chronically leaky roofs. The blocks do not have floors, only clay floors, so soft mud forms in the block, you have to slop through it the same way as outside in front of the block. Boots are rarities and the wooden clogs, get stuck and fall of the feet time after time. The women go around dressed mostly in old worn-out Soviet uniforms with scarfs on their shaven heads. The lucky ones are the owners of wooden shoes, as a rule a few sizes too large, which chafe the feet horribly (I know this from my own experience). Changes of underwear are incredibly rare, and when there are some they are dirty old rags. At first there were no sewers or water at all. So washing was not part of the program of camp duties. The women washed up in coffee or tea, which they had to buy from their comrades with bread."

From a report written by the Polish political prisoner Jerzy Tabeau after his escape from the camp in 1943.

Auschwitz II – Birkenau. Interior of a wooden barracks.

Auschwitz I. Over 400,000 prisoners were sent to the concentration camp and turned into modern slaves of the Third Reich, torn away from normal life and denied the most basic human rights and the principles of everyday life (Chronicle of the liberation of the camp, 1945).

From the memoirs written during the war by the Polish political prisoner Zofia Kossak-Szczucka.

"The lice, the scabies, and the lack of water were not the worst thing. There was one more nightmare. . . . It is impossible to remain silent about the everyday torment, repulsive and disgusting, caused by the latrines. They were in a small separate block. Down the middle ran a concrete perch, or bench, furnished with two rows of openings. . . . Next to the doors at both ends of the block, the stinking abyss of the sewer channel, uncovered and filled to the level of the floor, gaped open. Every so often, the "scheisskommando" emptied it. The supervisors were particularly abject hags . . . former prostitutes. . . . One latrine served several thousand women. Befouling the ground outside the latrine meant horrible punishment. Thus there were incredible scenes played out right at the entrance. Crowds of women fought desperately for a place, pushing each other into the repugnant pits. The clay soil around the block turned into deep mud, mixed with feces and urine. Some of the prisoners, exhausted with sickness, and especially the Greek women from the Salonika blocks, sank into it until they lost their thin wooden clogs and could not take a step. . . . The worst off were the ones suffering from diarrhea, and there was a multitude of them."

Auschwitz II – Birkenau. The interior of the latrine in a brick block. The inscription on the wall reads: "Maintain calm."

Auschwitz II – Birkenau.
The remains of a latrine in a wooden barracks that has been destroyed.

List of names of Jewish women prisoners selected in the camp as unfit for labor and sent to the gas chamber. Polish prisoners stole a copy of this list and sent it to a secret Polish resistance organization.

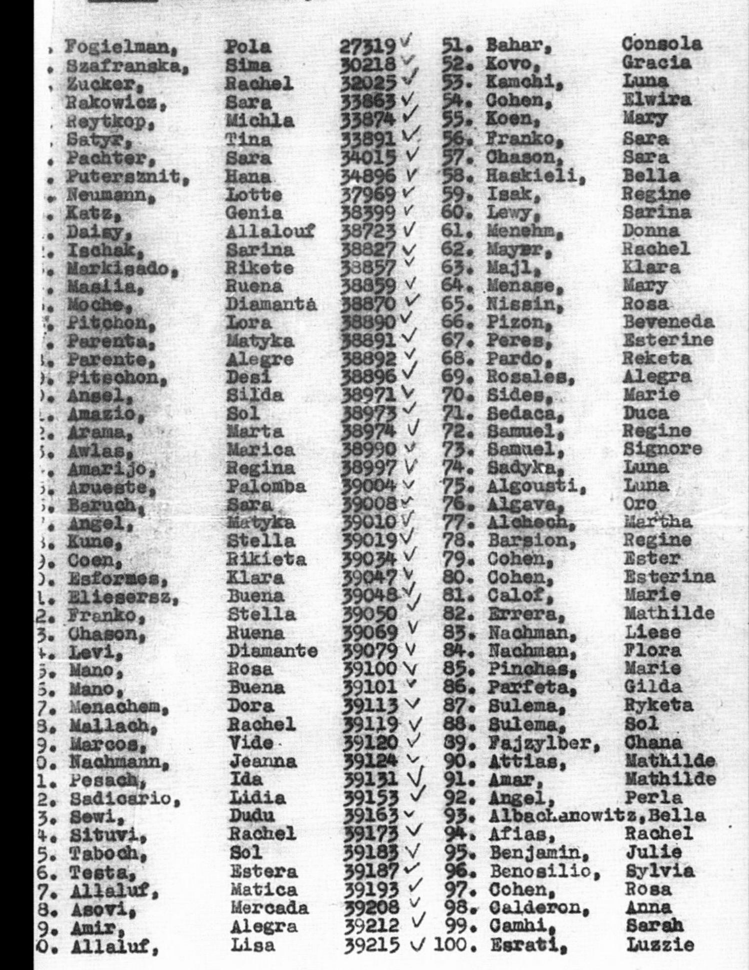

auen-Lager Birkenau
.: F.L.8.43.Ma-Krt.

Birkenau, den 21.Aug

Betr.: G.U.v.21.8.43.

Fogielman,	Pola	27319 ✓	51. Bahar,	Consola
Szafranska,	Sima	30218 ✓	52. Kovo,	Gracia
Zucker,	Rachel	32025 ✓	53. Kamchi,	Luna
Rakowicz,	Sara	33863 ✓	54. Cohen,	Elwira
Reytkop,	Michla	33874 ✓	55. Koen,	Mary
Satyr,	Tina	33891 ✓	56. Franko,	Sara
Pachter,	Sara	34015 ✓	57. Chason,	Sara
Puterssnit,	Hana	34896 ✓	58. Haskieli,	Bella
Neumann,	Lotte	37969 ✓	59. Isak,	Regine
Katz,	Genia	38399 ✓	60. Lewy,	Sarina
Daisy,	Allalouf	38723 ✓	61. Menehm,	Donna
Ischak,	Sarina	38827 ✓	62. Mayer,	Rachel
Markisado,	Rikete	38857 ✓	63. Majl,	Klara
Masiia,	Ruena	38859 ✓	64. Menase,	Mary
Moche,	Diamantá	38870 ✓	65. Nissin,	Rosa
Pitchon,	Lora	38890 ✓	66. Pizon,	Beveneda
Parenta,	Matyka	38891 ✓	67. Peres,	Esterine
Parente,	Alegre	38892 ✓	68. Pardo,	Reketa
Pitschon,	Desi	38896 ✓	69. Rosales,	Alegra
Ansel,	Silda	38971 ✓	70. Sides,	Marie
Amazio,	Sol	38973 ✓	71. Sedaca,	Duca
Arama,	Marta	38974 ✓	72. Samuel,	Regine
Awlas,	Marica	38990 ✓	73. Samuel,	Signore
Amarijo,	Regina	38997 ✓	74. Sadyka,	Luna
Arueste,	Palomba	39004 ✓	75. Algousti,	Luna
Baruch,	Sara	39008 ✓	76. Algava,	Oro
Angel,	Matyka	39010 ✓	77. Alchech,	Martha
Kune,	Stella	39019 ✓	78. Barsion,	Regine
Coen,	Rikieta	39034 ✓	79. Cohen,	Ester
Esformes,	Klara	39047 ✓	80. Cohen,	Esterina
Eliesersz,	Buena	39048 ✓	81. Calof,	Marie
Franko,	Stella	39050 ✓	82. Errera,	Mathilde
Chason,	Ruena	39069 ✓	83. Nachman,	Liese
Levi,	Diamante	39079 ✓	84. Nachman,	Flora
Mano,	Rosa	39100 ✓	85. Pinchas,	Marie
Mano,	Buena	39101 ✓	86. Parfeta,	Gilda
Menachem,	Dora	39113 ✓	87. Sulema,	Ryketa
Mallach,	Rachel	39119 ✓	88. Sulema,	Sol
Marcos,	Vide	39120 ✓	89. Fajzylber,	Chana
Nachmann,	Jeanna	39124 ✓	90. Attias,	Mathilde
Pesach,	Ida	39131 ✓	91. Amar,	Mathilde
Sadicario,	Lidia	39153 ✓	92. Angel,	Perla
Sewi,	Dudu	39163 ✓	93. Albachanowitz,	Bella
Situvi,	Rachel	39173 ✓	94. Afias,	Rachel
Taboch,	Sol	39183 ✓	95. Benjamin,	Julie
Testa,	Estera	39187 ✓	96. Benosilio,	Sylvia
Allaluf,	Matica	39193 ✓	97. Cohen,	Rosa
Asovi,	Mercada	39208 ✓	98. Calderon,	Anna
Amir,	Alegra	39212 ✓	99. Camhi,	Sarah
Allaluf,	Lisa	39215 ✓	100. Esrati,	Luzzie

They were photographed like criminals...

Digging foundations for new camp buildings.

Auschwitz II – Birkenau.
Part of the camp.

Auschwitz II – Birkenau. The road where women prisoners walked to work outside the camp.

Auschwitz II – Birkenau.
Barracks no. 25, referred to by prisoners as the Death Block.
"The group designated for liquidation leaves for the notorious block 25. That block is the antechamber to death. It serves the condemned as a last stage before the chamber, as a waiting room. . . . The selection usually lasts three or four days. Locked inside, the women receive nothing to eat or drink. Why should they? Their numbers have already been stricken off the books in the chancellery, and the fact that they are still alive is merely a saving of labor. Cattle at the slaughterhouse are not fed either. The unfortunate women were dying of thirst. They sobbed for water, begged for water. Dozens of hands reached out through the barred windows. . ."
From the memoirs written during the war by the Polish political prisoner Zofia Kossak-Szczucka.

Auschwitz II – Birkenau. The interior of a brick barracks where prisoners were crowded in by the hundreds.

Auschwitz I. Thousands of prisoners marched out through this gate every day to labor near the camp. They returned exhausted in the evening, carrying back to camp the bodies of those who died while working.

Auschwitz I. Block no. 10, where Professor Carl Clauberg, a German physician, carried out criminal experiments aimed at developing a method for sterilizing women rapidly and on a mass scale. He experimented on women prisoners, mostly Jewish. The wooden blinds on the windows were intended to prevent the women from observing prisoners being shot during the executions at the Death Wall.

"If my research continues as it has so far—and there is no reason to suppose that it will not—then we are not far from the moment when I will be able to say that a properly trained doctor in an appropriately equipped office, with perhaps ten auxiliary personnel, will probably be able to sterilize hundreds, or even a thousand persons, in a single day."

Professor Dr. Carl Clauberg, the German physician responsible for conducting sterilization experiments on women prisoners, in a June 7, 1943 letter to the Reichsführer SS, Heinrich Himmler.

Kochana Stefciu moja żonko
Już dzisiaj 31/10 idę niewinnie
na wykonanie pamiętaj zawsze
o mnie. Moja żonko a nasza
u Kochana Córeczkę wychowaj ją mi
w porządku i potemu żeby ją mi
Pan Jezus miał w swej opiece
gdy otrzymasz tę kartkę
pokaż ją Moi Mamie
Kochachana Mamo i Bracia i
siostry żyjcie w zgodzie i nie rów=
cie krzywdy moi Córce i Żonie.
Zostańcie z Panem Bogiem
i módlcie się za mnie

Jan Cupiał

adres
Cupiał Stefania
Trzebinia. Danczyngiera st. 6.

Farewell letter written covertly by a Pole sentenced to be shot, smuggled out of the camp to his family.

Auschwitz I.
The washroom where prisoners had to disrobe before being led naked to the Death Wall.

From the memoirs of Pery Broad, an SS man in the camp Gestapo: "A black wall was placed against the stone fence around the courtyard of Block no. 11. This wall was made out of black insulation panels, and it became the final milestone in the existence of thousands of innocent people: patriots who did not want to betray their fatherland for material advantage; prisoners who had managed to escape from the hell of Auschwitz, but whose bitter fate decreed that they should be captured . . . The *Rapportführer* or the jail supervisor did the shooting . . . Even though these were tottering skeletons, barely able to stand upright—some of them had vegetated for months in fetid underground cells that not even an animal could have endured—many shouted in their last seconds: 'Long live Poland!' or 'Long live freedom!' That is how Poles and Jews, constantly portrayed in Nazi propaganda as slaves whimpering for mercy, died."

Auschwitz I. The cellars of the Death Block. Punishment cells measuring 90 cm. x 90 cm., where four prisoners at a time were confined as a special penalty (partial reconstruction).

Auschwitz I. SS men observed prisoners through this spyhole.

Auschwitz I. The cellars of the Death Block.

Extract from the "Bunker Book," containing the records of the camp jail in the cellars of Block no. 11 (the death Block). The names of prisoners held in the jail are entered along with annotations about their subsequent fate. In many cases, a cross next to the date indicates their death. Dates of the executions of Polish officers and political activists in the camp resistance movement, among others, who were shot at the Death Wall.

Jude P	74345	Suchoflański Aron 1.1.23.- Skidel	"	† 21.9.43
Pol P	114789	Walter Bronislaw 26.4.97 - Gwizdziany	16.9.43 "	1.11.43
" "	2541	Jakubowski Tadeusz 30.8.08 - Warszawa	"	† 21.9.43
" "	20904	Baranowski Zbigniew 20.6.11 - Warszawa	"	28.9.43
Jude St	30519	Grossmann Adelbert 9.4.09 - Brzezany	"	† 21.9.43
Pol P	71886	Gilewicz Kazimierz 11.11.92 - Białopole	"	† 11.10.43
" "	329	Lisowski Tadeusz 23.7.09 - Myszyce	17.9.43 - "	† "

Image of the Crucifixion scratched in the wall of cell 21 in the Death Block.

Nr. 51o/1941

Auschwitz, den 19. August 1941.

Der Pfarrer Rajmund Kolbe, römisch-katholisch

wohnhaft Niepokalanow Kreis Sochaczew

ist am 14. August 1941 um 12 Uhr 50 Minuten

in Auschwitz, Kasernenstraße verstorben.

Der Verstorbene war geboren am 7. Januar 1894

in Zdunska Wola

(Standesamt Nr.)

Vater: Julius Kolbe

Mutter: Marie Kolbe geborene Dabrowski, wohnhaft in Krakau

~~Der Verstorbene war — nicht — verheiratet~~

Eingetragen auf ~~mündliche~~ — schriftliche Anzeige des Arztes Doktor Schwela in Auschwitz vom 14. August 1941

~~Der Anzeigende~~

~~Vorgelesen, genehmigt und unterschrieben~~

Die Übereinstimmung mit dem Erstbuch wird begiaubigt.

Auschwitz, den 19.8. 1941.

Der Standesbeamte
In Vertretung

Der Standesbeamte
In Vertretung
Grabner

Todesursache: Myocardinsuffizienz

Death certificate of Father Maksymilian (Rajmund) Kolbe, issued by the camp Civil Registry Office. The document gives a fictitious cause of death—coronary insufficiency.

Auschwitz I. The cellar of the Death Block. The starvation cell where Father Maksymilian (Rajmund) Kolbe died. The Roman Catholic Church canonized Father Kolbe on October 10, 1982.

Auschwitz I. Mieczysław Stobierski's sculpture "Starvation" in the permanent exhibition on camp conditions and starvation in Block no. 6.

Auschwitz II – Birkenau. Sector B II, built exclusively of wooden barracks.

Auschwitz, den 29. Juli 19 43

Der Straßenbautechniker Edmund Sikorski

katholisch,

wohnhaft Razias, Schirpserstraße Nr. 21,

ist am 19. Juli 1943 um 18 Uhr 20 Minuten

in Auschwitz, Kasernenstraße verstorben.

Der Verstorbene war geboren am 19. März 1920

in Czarnozin

(Standesamt Nr.)

Vater: Aleksander Sikorski, wohnhaft in Czarnozin

Mutter: Bronislawa Sikorski geborene Bogucki

D~~er Verstorbene war — nicht — verheiratet~~

Eingetragen auf ~~mündliche~~ — schriftliche Anzeige des Arztes Doktor der Medizin Kitt in Auschwitz vom 19. Juli 1943

~~D Anzeigende~~

~~Vorgelesen, genehmigt und unterschrieben.~~

Die Übereinstimmung mit dem Erstbuch wird beglaubigt.

Auschwitz, den 29.7. 1943

Der Standesbeamte
In Vertretung

Der Standesbeamte
In Vertretung
Grabner

Todesursache: Plötzlicher Herztod

A public execution was conducted on a specially erected mass gallows during camp roll call on July 19, 1943. Ten Polish prisoners were executed on suspicion of aiding three escapees and of having contact with Polish civilians living near Oświęcim. Despite the fact that a great many prisoners witnessed this execution, a fictitious cause of death was listed in the death certificates issued for the victims by the camp Civil Registry Office: *plötzlicher Herztod* (sudden coronary arrest).

Auschwitz I. The portable gallows where prisoners were hanged.

Auschwitz I. The "goat," where prisoners were flogged. The official penalty was 25 lashes. However, cases are known where up to 70 lashes were inflicted.

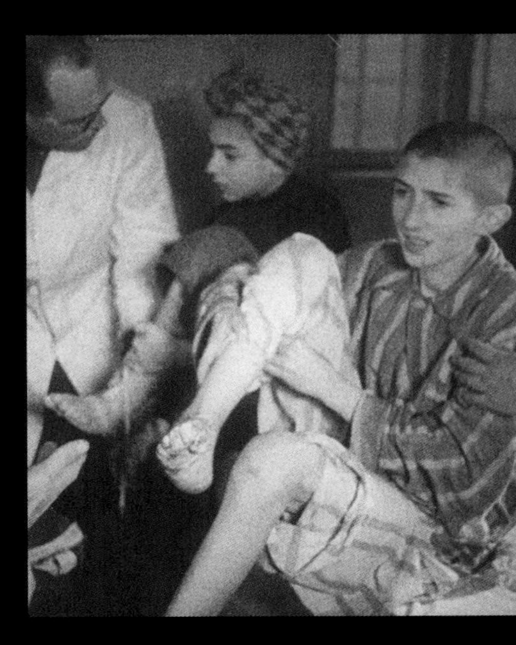

Children with frostbitten feet, subjected to the "standing penalty" (Chronicle of the liberation of the camp, 1945).

Konz.-Lager Auschwitz
Abteilung III

Birkenau
~~Auschwitz~~, den 26. August 1943

Meldung

Ich melde den, ~~die~~ K a l m a n , Aba, geb. 8.12.1924 zu Zakroczym

~~Schutz — , Vorb. — , Aso. — , Bv.~~ — , Juden — , Häftling Nr. 8o 498

weil er, ~~sie~~ am 2o.8.1943 über den Draht zum Zigeunerlager Päckchen hinübergeworfen hat.

Strafe bekanntgegeben
... X. 1943
[signature]
SS Ustuf.

Strafe: 2 mal Stehzelle
1o mal Strafarbeit

Der 1. Schutzhaftlagerführer
[signature]
SS-Hauptsturmführer

Gesehen u. weitergeleitet:
Der 1. Schutzhaftlagerführer
[signature]
SS-Hauptsturmführer

5. OKT. 1943

Josef Schillinger
Vor- u. Zuname
SS-Unterscharführer
Dienstgrad

A punishment report: Kalman Aba, a Jew, was punished with two nights' confinement in the standing bunker and ten days of penal labor for passing something into the Gypsy camp.

Konz. - Lager Auschwitz III
Abteilung III

Monowitz, den 5.2.44.

95

Strafverfügung
abgesandt am 7. Feb. 1944

Meldung

Ich melde den, ~~die~~ E n g e l Josef, geb. 8.6.18. zu Pabianice

poln. Schutz—, ~~Vorb.—, Aso.—, Bv.~~—, Juden—, Häftling Nr. 159 344

weil er, ~~sie~~ einen Selbstmordversuch unternommen hat, indem er sich mit einem Messer eine Schnittwunde am Halse beigebracht hat. Er wurde von dem Häftling Nr. 70 795 im Schacht, in einer toten Strecke, in einer Blutlache liegend aufgefunden und sofort in den Häftlings-Krankenbau überführt, wo sich herausgestellt hat, daß seine Verletzung nicht lebensgefährlich ist.
(Arbeitslager Jawischowitz, Revier 7 - Kohlenförderung.)

25

Strafe: 25 Stockhiebe.

Gesehen u. weitergeleitet:
Der 1. Schutzhaftlagerführer
Schöttl
SS-Obersturmführer

[signature]
Vor- u. Zuname
SS-Unterscharführer.
Dienstgrad

A punishment report: Josef Engel, a Polish Jew, attempted to commit suicide by cutting his throat with a knife while laboring in a coal mine. He was punished by flogging.

The corpses of prisoners who died or were murdered in the last days of Auschwitz Concentration Camp are taken away.

The fence around the camp (Auschwitz I and Auschwitz II – Birkenau) was almost fourteen kilometers long.

Auschwitz I. Guard towers
and the double camp fence.

Auschwitz II – Birkenau. The corpses of prisoners, which the SS had not managed to burn, were found when the camp was liberated. A ceremonial burial was held near the camp (Photograph by Henryk Makarewicz).

Auschwitz II – Birkenau. Part of the camp.

Auschwitz II – Birkenau. After liberation (Chronicle of the liberation of the camp).

Auschwitz II – Birkenau. Newly arrived Jews from Hungary at the railroad ramp, before being sent to the gas chamber (SS photo, 1944).

Auschwitz II – Birkenau. Newly arrived Jewish women, selected on the ramp as capable of labor, their heads already shaved, being sent to the camp (SS photo, 1944).

Auschwitz II – Birkenau. The wall of remembrance presenting family photographs brought to the camp by Polish Jews deported here.

Państwowe Muzeum Auschwitz – Birkenau
ul. Więźniów Oświęcimia 20
PL 32-603 Oświęcim
e-mail: muzeum@auschwitz.org.pl
www.auschwitz.org.pl

Biały Kruk Sp. z o.o.
ul. Szwedzka 38
PL 30-324 Kraków
tel. +48 12/ 260 32 40, 260 32 90
e-mail: biuro@bialykruk.pl
www.bialykruk.pl

First Edition, Kraków – Oświęcim 2003
ISBN 83-88918-26-5